Understanding ERISA

A Compact Guide to the Landmark Act

Compliments of
Thornburg Investment Management

BY KEN ZIESENHEIM, CFP, JD, LL.M

President, Thornburg Securities Corporation

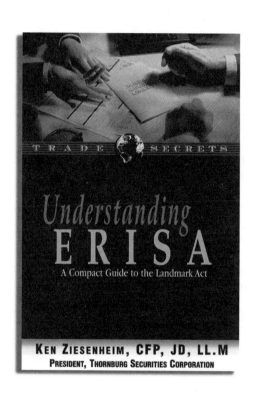

TRADE SECRETS

Understanding ERISA
A Compact Guide to the Landmark Act

KEN ZIESENHEIM, CFP, JD, LL.M
PRESIDENT, THORNBURG SECURITIES CORPORATION

This publication is designed to provide accurate and authoritative
information in regard to the subject matter covered. It is sold with the
understanding that neither the author nor the publisher is engaged in
rendering legal, accounting, or other professional service. If legal advice or
other expert assistance is required, the services of a competent professional
person should be sought.

This handbook is not intended to be used as a legal opinion. You should
discuss how to apply these issues to your circumstances with an attorney
knowledgeable in this area of the law.

*From a Declaration of Principles jointly adopted by a Committee of the
American Bar Association and a Committee of Publishers.*

Technical editorial assistance provided by: Larry Chambers

This book, along with other books, are available at discounts
that make it realistic to provide them as gifts to your customers,
clients, and staff. For more information on these long lasting, cost
effective premiums, please call John Boyer at 800-424-4550 or
email him at john@traderslibrary.com.

ISBN 1-931611-42-4

Printed in the United States of America.

TABLE OF CONTENTS

Chapter 20

FOREWORD

Compliance with the Employee Retirement and Income Security Act (ERISA) rules has been a major concern of trustees and plan sponsors since this landmark legislation was passed in 1974. The scope and complexity of ERISA has led to a widespread lack of understanding of its basic principles and a commensurate lack of understanding of liabilities to which trustees and fiduciaries may be subjected.

These rules, governed by the Department of Labor (DOL), impose heavy responsibilities on any persons involved in the management of employee benefit plans. Unfortunately, many trustees and advisors are not aware of the responsibilities, liabilities and penalties under ERISA until they find themselves in violation of the Act.

This booklet has been prepared to clarify the issues surrounding ERISA. It will provide trustees, advisors and fiduciaries charged with the responsibility of managing pension plan assets guidelines for compliance with the complex maze of ERISA rules. Most importantly, it offers a framework to assist in the development of a system of conformity, which will enable them to fulfill their fiduciary obligations. Financial advisors will find it particularly useful in establishing compliance procedures for their practices. And the compact format and sample forms will make the concepts easy to implement.

ERISA was enacted to protect the interests of participants in employee benefit plans from abuses and discriminatory practices. ERISA was also adopted to tie together both trust law principles and the special nature and purpose of employee benefit plans. It had, as one of its central purposes, a public policy of ensuring adequate investment returns necessary to provide secure retirements for defined benefit plan participants.

While based in large part on traditional principles of trust law, ERISA recognizes the limitations of these principles in portfolio management. Departing somewhat from the Prudent Man Rule, ERISA sets a standard of prudence to govern pension investments that is more attuned with economic reality and important academic developments in investment theory. The Act fundamentally changed trust investment law from procedural to more process-oriented.

The American Law Institute's 1992 Restatement (Third) of Trusts restated the legal principles which govern trust investments for the purpose of reconciling trust investment law with changes in investment practices. The Restatement (Third)'s revised standard of prudent investment is known as the Prudent Investor Rule and follows the innovations of ERISA. This rule will be presented, along with the effects of the Uniform Prudent Investor Act of 1994.

The intention here is to impart knowledge and confidence so that, by implementing and maintaining the standards outlined in this booklet, trustees/fiduciaries can actually attain the greatest value for their plans while providing the necessary safeguards and protections to plan participants. It is also hoped that the concise nature of this booklet and the forms enclosed will make it far more convenient for all who need to be in compliance with ERISA – as well as those who need to know what standards their trustees or fiduciaries must be held to – as they attempt to understand the issues and conform to them.

These rules apply to all qualified plans including defined benefit plans, defined contribution plans, 401(k) plans, 403(b) plans, IRA's and others.

Harold Evensky,
Evensky Group

✳✳✳✳✳

Mr. Evensky is Chairman of the Evensky Group, Private Family Offices. Harold serves on the TIAA-CREF Institute advisory board; is a member of the FPA, the Academy of Financial Services, AIMR and is an associate member of the American Bar Association. he is also the acclaimed author "Wealth Management: The Financial Advisor's Guide to Investing & Managing Your Client's Assets."

Notes:

[1] H.R. Rep. No. 1280, 93rd Cong., 2d Session 302.

INTRODUCTION

Prior to ERISA, a company could have a pension fund that wasn't really backed by anything. If the company wasn't profitable or went out of business, the pension evaporated and participants suffered. In those days, there were no 401(k)s, and IRA's hadn't been invented. For retirement, most people relied on a pension plan, even though few truly understood how the plans worked, or where the money was coming from. They just assumed their company was going to pay them a certain amount of money per year after they retired.

Since there was no oversight of pension plans, there were abuses. The system was out of control, so, in 1974, the federal government enacted the Employee Retirement and Income Security Act (ERISA). The Act mandated that it was unfair for an employee to work at a company for 20 or 30 years and then lose their retirement benefits. Employers were required to fund their retirement plans, putting money aside so that if the company went bankrupt, employees were still guaranteed pensions.

The Act outlined rules and determined how much money must be allocated for pension funds based on how many employees a corporation had. It further stipulated that anything done with this pool of money must be for the benefit of the employees. As that became the only consideration, it eliminated the inherent conflict of interest that results when a company tries to serve itself and its retirees at the same time.

Standard employee retirement plans now include profit-sharing, pension and 401(k)s. However, any plan maintained by an employer for the benefit of employees is covered by ERISA, including stock bonus plans, insurance plans (life, health and disability), and vacation and scholarship funds.

ERISA also provides a federal standard of conduct to be followed and observed concerning the management of retirement fund assets:

> *Anyone who is a trustee, sponsor or otherwise exercises any authority or control over any type of employee benefit plan is a fiduciary. The fiduciary should act with the "care, skill, prudence, and diligence under the circumstances then prevailing that a prudent man acting in a like capacity and familiar with such matters would use in the conduct of an enterprise of like character and with like aims." (ERISA Sec. 404(a)(1)(B))*

A fiduciary not only has a duty to become familiar with ERISA and to follow its standards, but also to seek outside assistance when appropriate. It is extremely important for all plan fiduciaries to understand the scope of their responsibilities and the potential penalties for shirking their responsibilities under ERISA. A fiduciary can be held personally liable for breach or violation of these responsibilities, even to the extent of having to restore lost profits to the plan.[2]

The scope of the fiduciary responsibility is much wider than generally recognized because the ERISA definition of fiduciary is so broad. To be considered a fiduciary, one must only have an element of authority or control over the plan, including plan management, administration or disposition of assets, or any person who renders investment advice to a plan for a fee.

Notes:

[2] The pension trustees who breached the fiduciary duties of this plan were jointly and severally liable for more than $2 million plus interest, costs and legal fees. Katsaros vs. Cody (DC E NY, 12/27/83)

Chapter 1

FIDUCIARY CONDUCT

Every fiduciary is responsible for knowing the "prudent requirements" for the investment of retirement plan assets. A fiduciary not acting in accordance with the precepts of ERISA could subject the plan under management to loss of its tax-free status. Unfortunately, obtaining information and guidance in this area has been difficult.

Until recently, the investment authority of trustees in most states was governed by a standard known as the **Prudent Man Rule**. The Prudent Man doctrine traces its origin to the early eighteenth century when the courts defined the conduct of a fiduciary as one who was responsible for managing someone else's money. Under common law, an individual who claims to have superior skills is held to a higher legal standard; i.e., the Prudent Expert standard.

ERISA holds fiduciaries to standards as high as those for a professional money manager or investment expert when it comes to making investment decisions.[3] A good argument can be made that professional money managers, investment advisors, banks, and trust companies (who serve as qualified plan fiduciaries) hold themselves out to be experts, and are, therefore, subject to ERISA's Prudent Expert rule.[4] This is apparent from the case law.

ERISA does recognize degrees of professionalism, depending on the size of the plan's assets. For example, an unpaid fiduciary of a plan with a small amount of assets is, arguably, judged differently from a plan with a large amount of assets. Therefore, if the size and nature of the plan would indicate the need for an experienced manager, the fiduciary should not be heard to plead his lack of expertise after his investments go sour. The fiduciary is required to at least be familiar with pension investment management, or to seek help from a qualified professional.

Notes:

[3] Klevan, "Fiduciary Responsibility Under ERISA's Prudent Man Rule: What Are the Guideposts?" 44 J. of Taxation 153, 154.

[4] Klevan, supra at 154.

Chapter 2

LIABILITIES AND PENALTIES

Any fiduciary that breaches ERISA's fiduciary obligations can be held personally liable for losses caused by that breach of duty. As discussed earlier, the definition of a fiduciary is broad and the responsibilities are not mitigated by simply delegating fiduciary duties.[5]

Moreover, fiduciaries may be personally liable if they know, or should have known of, a breach by another fiduciary. Pleading ignorance, bad communications or inexperience will not be adequate legal defenses. Delegation to prudent experts and the proper overseeing of them are the only defenses upon which a fiduciary can rely.

ERISA makes no provision for punitive damages, but it does provide for the assessment of a penalty against a fiduciary of 20 percent for any amount recovered as a result of an ERISA violation.[6]

> *"Any person who is a fiduciary with respect to a plan who breaches any of the responsibilities, obligations, or duties imposed upon fiduciaries by this title shall be personally liable to make good to such plan any profits*

of such fiduciary which have been made through use of assets of the plan by the fiduciary, and shall be subject to such other equitable or remedial relief as the court may deem appropriate, including removal of such fiduciary." (ERISA Sec. 409[a])

Penalties may be imposed for up to six years after the fiduciary violation, or three years after the party-bringing suit had knowledge of the breach. A willful violation carries personal criminal penalties of up to $5,000 ($100,000 for corporations) and up to one year in prison.

Losses to the plan, as well as profits made from the improper use of plan assets, must be restored to the plan. Failure to disclose information to plan participants can result in daily monetary penalties. The Department of Labor can also remove the fiduciary and take control over plan assets.

Civil actions can be initiated by plan participants, beneficiaries, other fiduciaries and/or the Department of Labor. As participants become more knowledgeable about their rights (and more sophisticated about invest-ment alternatives) lawsuits will undoubtedly increase.

Notes:

[5] The fact that trustees may have acted with good intentions or in good faith is no defense if their conduct did not meet the objective standard. Donovan vs. Mazzoia (DC N CAL 11/17/81)

[6] ERISA Sec. 502(1). See also, "Report to the Secretary of the Task Force on enforcement (9-90), relating to the ERISA Enforcement Strategy Implementation Plan.

Chapter 3

GOVERNMENTAL AGENCIES

Three governmental agencies—the Department of Labor (DOL), Internal Revenue Service (IRS), and Pension Benefit Guaranty Corporation (PBGC)—oversee retirement plan compliance with various rules and regulations. The DOL has the primary responsibility for promulgating and enforcing fiduciary compliance. Because of the tax-deferred status of qualified plans and Individual Retirement Accounts, and their interplay with general tax compliance, the IRS oversees participation, vesting and funding standards. The PBGC ensures that defined benefit plans (future retirement benefit is fixed, current contribution by sponsor is not) are properly funded to meet current and future obligations.[7]

DOL and IRS auditors and investigators are authorized to examine retirement plans for compliance, and recently have become more concerned about problems. When a problem or violation is detected, an enforcement action can be brought against the fiduciaries of the plan.

Remedial actions for ERISA violations include:

1. Recoupment of investment losses.

2. Disgorgement of profits.

3. Payment of the difference between actual investment returns and the returns that could have been achieved from reasonably prudent investment alternatives.

4. Preliminary and permanent injunctive relief.

5. Removal of a fiduciary and appointment of a receiver.

6. Disqualification of the tax deferred status of the plan.[8]

Notes:

[7] See PBGC v. LTV. 110 S. Ct. 2668 (1990).

[8] ERISA Sec. 401.

Chapter 4

PRUDENT INVESTOR RULE

The American Law Institute's work restates the basic rule governing the investment of assets of a trust, known as the prudent investment rule. The formulation of the prudent investment rule affords more latitude for trustees to excerise judgment than was thought to be permitted by the Restatement Second of Trusts. The revised rule focuses on the trust's portfolio as a whole and the investment strategy on which it is based, rather than viewing a specific investment in isolation.

The restatement is a guide for practitioners of law, trustees and investment advisers, as well as a source of legal authority.

The 1974 ERISA and its 1979 regulations did not tell corporations how to manage their money, but it did state that the trustees of the corporations' pension funds are fiduciaries and mandated that they be guided by the **Prudent Investor Rule**. The fiduciary is under a duty to the beneficiaries to invest and manage the funds of the trust as a prudent investor would, in light of the purposes, terms, distribution requirements, and other circumstances of the trust.

The Prudent Investor Rule states that any investment selection may be made, provided that a review of the decision at a later date would determine that, with the information available at the time, the choice was a prudent one. While it didn't give specifics, the Rule gave enough guidance so that corporations knew they'd better have an audit trail and that their decisions had better make sense, even to someone looking at them 10 or 20 years in the future. If any employee later claimed that he or she didn't get the pension they were entitled to, the corporation would be able to prove that, given the circumstances at the time, their actions were prudent.

ERISA recognized the need for departures from traditional applications of the Prudent Man Rule of trust law. This is indicated, in part, by the U.S. Department of Labor recognizing regulations of modern portfolio theory and of more flexible concepts (for example, in delegation and in risk-return relationships). Heavy emphasis in the regulations on the duty of loyalty and prohibited transactions (even for otherwise prudent, profitable investments) is understandable in this context. Likewise, there exists the possibility of an interpretation that imposes a standard of skill in investment management different from that imposed by general trust law.[9]

Conflicts Between The Prudent-Man Rule And Modern Asset Management Practices:

Investment products and techniques have developed and changed over the years. So have information and theories concerning financial markets and prudent investing, backed by extensive research and by the authoritative judgments and investment behavior patterns of expert fund managers.

The Prudent Investor Rule seeks to modernize trust investment law and to restore the generality and flexibility of the original doctrine. The language of the Prudent Investor Rule is intended to preserve the law's adaptability by confining its mandates to those that seem essential to prudence (based on traditional duties of care, skill, and caution), to the protection of fiduciary goals, and to supplying helpful guidance to courts and fiduciaries.

This goal calls for a limited body of legal rules that draw upon the consistent themes of legitimate theories and express only those principles upon which there is general agreement. This much is needed in order to protect trust beneficiaries and meet objectives, while also providing standards by which to judge and guide a fiduciary's conduct. Yet, the rules must be general and flexible enough to adapt to changes in the financial world and to permit sophisticated, prudent use of any investments and courses of action that are suitable to the purposes and circumstances of the diverse trusts.

Thus, the objectives of the Prudent Investor Rule range from "liberating expert trustees to pursue challenging, rewarding, non-traditional strategies when appropriate to the particular trust" to "providing other trustees with reasonably clear guidance to safe harbors that are practical, adaptable, readily identifiable, and expectedly rewarding."

Notes:

[9] ERISA 404, 29 U.S.C., pg. 66, Restatement of the Law Third, The American Law Institute, Trusts, Prudent Investor Rule.

Chapter 5

UNIFORM PRUDENT INVESTOR ACT

In 1994, the National Conference of Commissioners on State Laws approved a model state statute incorporating the principles of the Restatement (Third) of Trusts, 1992, into the Uniform Prudent Investor Act (UPIA).

The 1994 UPIA fundamentally changes trust investment law. It emphasizes the interplay between risk and reward in the portfolio as a whole. Traditional trust law emphasizes the duty to "preserve principal" at all costs and to avoid "speculation." Because each investment was considered on its own merits without regard to the portfolio as a whole, a fiduciary could become a guarantor of risky investments, even if it picked many more winners than losers.

Under the UPIA, a fiduciary must first determine the appropriate risk profile for a trust, then develop and implement an investment strategy for the portfolio. It must be able to justify the reasonableness of that strategy and the prudence of each investment as it relates thereto.

Major Points

1. The standard of prudence applies to the trust as a whole rather than to individual investments, with a realization that particular investments that would have been viewed as speculative and subject to surcharge under old law may be sensible, risk-reducing additions to a portfolio viewed as a whole.

2. The overall investment strategy should be based upon risk and reward objectives suitable for the trust. These objectives will vary widely, depending on the circumstances in each trust arrangement. Trusts will be concerned with preserving the real purchasing power of the trust and the effects of inflation on that power, a factor that was often ignored under prior law.

3. No particular investment is inherently prudent or imprudent. The premise of the rule is that trust beneficiaries are better protected by increasing the fiduciary's responsibilities and powers than by per se restrictions or safe harbors.

4. A corporate fiduciary or paid professional advisor acting as fiduciary is accountable under a special investment skills standard.

5. Delegation is permitted, encouraged and, in some cases, required. The UPIA reverses the anti-delegation rule of prior law. This change recognizes that prudent investing may require the use of outside expertise in some circumstances by

both professionals and non-professionals.

6. The fiduciary's liability for improper conduct will be measured by reference to the total return that should have been expected from an appropriate investment program. Thus, a positive return will not necessarily protect a fiduciary from liability.

The Uniform Prudent Investor Act and Modern Portfolio Theory

The UPIA is clearly the result of a consensus about the significance of modern portfolio theory and the realization that the law and the markets should have similar views regarding prudent investment practices. The UPIA is a process-oriented rule; it is not merely procedural. As the Restatement (Third) makes clear, a fiduciary that strays from the basic tenets of modern portfolio theory must carry a burden of persuasion as to the reasonableness of his or her actions.

Modern portfolio theory refers to the process of reducing risk in a portfolio through systematic diversification across asset classes and within a particular asset class. It involves the relationship between risk and reward. It assumes that all investors desire the highest possible returns while bearing the lowest amount of risk, and that public markets are generally efficient. To increase the return, an investor must incur more risk.

A well-diversified portfolio minimizes the risk that a particular investment will not perform well (firm-specific risk) and leaves a portfolio exposed only to market risk. Investors without an efficiently diversified portfolio are exposed to unnecessary risk, which will not be compensated by the market.

Here's the point: There is disagreement about the degree of efficiency of public markets. Thus, modern portfolio theory and the UPIA allow for many alternative strategies to assemble an optimal portfolio along what is called the "efficient frontier," which maximizes potential returns at the desired level of risk.

Effects on a fiduciary's liabilities

A fiduciary can choose any investment for a trust and not be responsible for the performance of the investments if the fiduciary has properly conducted the process required by the UPIA.

The UPIA assesses the fiduciary's liability by the investment process, not the outcome.[10] Under prior law, the investment process was also an important element in assessing fiduciary liability, but evidence of careful deliberation was usually sufficient to protect a fiduciary, as long as the fiduciary had avoided investments that could be deemed "speculative."

However, the process required by the UPIA includes important substantive elements. A fiduciary must be familiar with modern portfolio theory to conduct the process. A fiduciary that does not incorporate these concepts into its investment process probably will not be saved by an otherwise impressive paper trail.

The UPIA Section 2(f) charges a fiduciary with special

skills or expertise to use those skills or expertise. This is familiar law, but the comment thereto implies that all professional trustees will be held to a single high standard that will not vary by location or amount of assets under management. The notion seems to be that the basic tools and knowledge necessary to manage risk in a professional manner are available to any professional, wherever located. Smaller organizations in rural locations will probably be held to the same standards as their larger counterparts.

The UPIA's protection from liability depends upon the fiduciary's ability to demonstrate that it has met this heightened standard. A fiduciary is at risk, even with a positive return, if the fiduciary cannot demonstrate that it conducted a thorough and ongoing process for each trust, incorporating the current standards in the investment management industry (including risk and return assessment and efficient portfolio selection).

This process imposes considerable new responsibilities on professional trustees, and is a significant departure from prior law.

Recognition of risk/return relationships

The UPIA recognizes that the key task of the fiduciary is to manage risk in order to realize the trust's objectives. The UPIA Official Commentary states that Section 2 is "the heart of the Act" and that it is intended to sound "the main theme of modern investment practice: sensitivity to the risk/return curve."

Prior law emphasized the avoidance of risk, but modern portfolio theory has established that, without risk, there will be no rewards. The UPIA requires a fiduciary to take on the level of risk appropriate to the trust and to manage the risk.[11]

Risk is managed through efficient diversification. Trust law has long required it. However, prior law required little more than not putting all your eggs in one basket. UPIA Section 3 greatly enhances the duty of diversification. It is clear that the Restatement (Third) and the UPIA require that diversification be systematic, and that it eliminate uncompensated risk.

A fiduciary cannot simply label a trust as having a "conservative" risk profile and proceed accordingly. It must conduct and document a process to gather, record and analyze information about each trust's time horizons, cash flow needs, risk aversion, tax status, intentions and other factors, not only at the trust's inception, but on an ongoing basis. A primary purpose of this exercise is to generate the information necessary for a fiduciary to determine the "efficient frontier" for each trust. The fiduciary must be prepared to carry a burden to justify each investment, in relation to a portfolio strategy that the fiduciary has developed, as suitable for the risk level appropriate to each particular trust.

The fiduciary's investment process under the UPIA can be viewed in three steps: (1) evaluate the needs and purposes of the trust and determine the appropriate risk level; (2) develop an overall investment strategy having risk and return objectives reasonably suitable to the trust; and (3) implement that policy through a strategy of selecting individual investments.

Notes:

[10] 1994 the National Conference of Commissioners on State Laws.

[11] ibid.

Chapter 6

PRUDENT INVESTMENT PROCEDURES

The General Standard of Prudent Investment Procedures was originally formulated as a general statement that would allow fiduciaries the flexibility appropriate to particular circumstances. This standard requires that reasonable care, skill, and caution be applied to investments, not in isolation, but in the context of the trust portfolio and as a part of an overall investment strategy, which should incorporate risk and return objectives reasonably suitable to the trust.

In essence, the fiduciary must: (1) conform to fundamental fiduciary duties of loyalty and impartiality; (2) act with prudence in deciding whether and how to delegate authority and in the selection and supervision of agents; and (3) incur only costs that are reasonable in amount and appropriate to the investment responsibilities of the trusteeship.

These are the steps, which must be taken by a fiduciary that invests plan assets:

1. The qualified plan must establish a written inves-

ment policy and that policy must be followed. ERISA Sections 402(b)(1) and 404(A)(1)(D).

2. The qualified plan assets must be diversified, unless, under the circumstances it is clearly not prudent to do so. ERISA Section 404(a)(1)(C).

3. Qualified plan investments must be made according to ERISA Prudent Man requirements. ERISA Section 404(a)(1)(B).

4. The performance of qualified plan investments must be monitored and reviewed. ERISA Section 405(a) provides that a fiduciary may be held personally liable to the plan for all losses. Arguably, the review should be more frequent than once every three to five year market cycle.

5. Qualified plan investment expenses must be reasonable. ERISA Section 404(a).

6. A qualified plan investment must not result in a direct or indirect prohibited transaction. ERISA Section 406.

Each fiduciary must assume that his (her) investment decisions will be examined in detail in the future.[12] Documentation is critical and spans a wide array of both internal and external reporting requirements. Internal record-keeping functions require building an audit file that can be quickly produced and reviewed to verify compliance. External reports are required to satisfy plan participants and regulatory authorities.

The following supporting documentation should be maintained regarding decisions that are made:

1. Journals, ledgers, account statements (including bank and trust statements), appraisals, etc., that support all plan assets/investments.

2. Analysis and reports from investment managers, consultants and performance measurement data.

3. Certificates, documents, statements of additional information (if a mutual fund), confirmations and any and all necessary items depicting evidence of ownership in the plan's assets/investments.

4. Annual copies of Form ADV for each money manager, along with certification by the manager that appropriate registrations under the Investment Advisors Act of 1940 and the State Securities Board are maintained. In addition, the manager should certify that there is no material litigation pending against the manager that involves allegations of a breach of fiduciary duty or securities law violations.

5. Proof of satisfaction of the ERISA bonding requirements for all fiduciaries (including money managers and trustees) dealing with plan assets.[13]

6. A detailed report of investment transaction turnover, costs, fees and expenses.

Notes:

[12] Procedural Prudence, Donald B. Trone, William R. Allbright
[13] "Every fiduciary of an employee benefit plan and every person who handles funds or other property of such a plan...shall be bonded as provided in this section." (ERISA Sec. 412(a)).

Chapter 7

WRITTEN INVESTMENT POLICY

The written investment policy statement is a critical first step in building a structure for ERISA conformity. A written investment policy statement enables you to clearly define your preferred investment methodology and communicate long-term goals and objectives. It serves as a framework for allocating the assets among various investment classes, hiring investment mangers and monitoring performance.

A. Definition

An Investment Policy Statement is a written statement that sets forth the investment objectives of the pension fund portfolio and general guidelines for specific investment decisions. This Statement should provide specific instructions to an investment counselor and cover such topics as target rates of return, risk tolerance, any short fall makeup, anticipated withdrawals or contributions, regulatory issues and desired holding periods of asset classes:

1. The fund's investment objective (e.g., aggressive growth, conservative growth, income, etc.);

2. The fund's liquidity requirements (i.e., cash equivalents needed);

3. The marketability of the pension fund investments;

4. The quality of the pension fund investments (bond and security ratings);

5. The level of turnover or trading action allowable;

6. The rate of return to be achieved;

7. The time period for measuring investment performance;

8. The risk constraints and other restrictions to be placed on the investment manager.

It should be noted that the plan's portfolio mix will not exactly conform to the ideal mix for that investment objective because of changes in the market, economy, etc.

B. Reasons for an Investment Policy Statement

The three main reasons why a qualified plan sponsor needs to establish a clear investment policy are: (1) to help meet pension plan objectives (i.e., meeting retirement benefit obligations due participants; thereby, making it more likely that the fund will support and contribute to the value of the plan sponsor); (2) to satisfy regulatory and legal requirements (e.g., the Prudent Man rule and a procedure to satisfy ERISA section 402(b)(1)'s funding requirements); and, (3) to establish effective communication with investment managers..

C. Fiduciary responsibility for developing an Investment Policy Statement

Normally, the investment manager, trustee, or plan sponsor (or possibly all three) are responsible for developing the Investment Policy Statement. Yet, their knowledge of investment markets may be scarcely better than the average participant in the plan. It is critical, then, that the fiduciary obtains unbiased objective input and guidance from appropriate advisors in order to properly fulfill his or her role. It is not uncommon for the fiduciary to take a "crash course" on investment alternatives and market cycles before preparing the investment policy statement.

The interpretation can be made that a financial advisor who helps develop a plan's Investment Policy Statement is an ERISA fiduciary ("functional fiduciary") i.e., provides individualized investment advice for a fee on an ongoing basis.

D. Qualitative aspects

At a minimum, the following items should be covered when designing an Investment Policy Statement:

1. The type of plan (defined benefit, defined contribution, profit sharing, etc.), date of adoption, and number of employees covered;

2. The current dollar value of the assets to be managed and assumptions as to the projected cash inflows (from contributions) and projected out-

flows (from withdrawals) over the ensuing years (e.g., three, five and 10 years);

3. Cash flow of the plan (both in and out) — liquidity requirements;

4. The accrued and projected liabilities of the plan which may change the funding status (over or underfunded) as the plan's assumptions and/or investment performance and participant demographics change;

5. The stability of earnings by the plan sponsor and the ability of the sponsor to sustain contributions;

6. The investment objectives the plan must attain in order to meet funding objectives and/or the overall return objective for plan assets (e.g., three percent over Consumer Price Index). Plan assets must not be used for any other objectives, such as using the assets in corporate takeover activities;

7. Asset classes appropriate for the plan (based on risk tolerances, correlation and time horizon), and permitted by regulations.

8. Nominal return benchmarks (with consideration of the "real" rate of return).

9. Definition of "risk";

10. The plan's tolerance for risk and volatility of returns, consistent with the plan's funding policy;

11. The percentage mix of asset classes that will yield the highest probability of meeting long-term investment objectives without exceeding tolerances for short-term volatility;

12. How investment decisions will be made, and if money managers will be hired, how they will be selected. Procedure for selecting and dismissing money managers;

13. How the plan's portfolio performance will be monitored and how money managers will be supervised, including appropriate benchmark indices (e.g., S&P 500 Index for domestic equity managers);

14. Time period for review and evaluation. Procedures should be established to periodically review performance compared to the investment policy statement and amend or change objectives, as necessary.

The plan document does not have to be overly complex, as long as the objectives are specific enough to meet the plan's needs and goals. Some very comprehensive Investment Policy Statements have been contained within three pages.

Written objectives are as integral to a three-person pension plan as they are to massive employee plans. Fiduciaries in both cases will be held to standards defined by ERISA, as well as those defined by plan documents.

Chapter 8

SAMPLE: INVESTMENT POLICY STATEMENT

XYZ Company, Inc.
PROFIT-SHARING PLAN

This Investment Policy Statement shall provide the trustees of XYZ Company, Inc. Profit-Sharing Plan with the principles and guidelines on which all future decisions relating to the management of the assets in the XYZ Company, Inc., Profit-Sharing Plan shall be managed.

PLAN DATA

Employees Covered: All employees of XYZ Company, Inc., with service to the company of more than one year, and whose time and service during the year is at least 1000 hours. As of December 1, 2000, there were 95 employees of XYZ Company, Inc., of which 50 were eligible participants in the plan.

Vesting Schedule		
Years of Service	**Vested Percentage**	**Forfeited Percentage**
Less than 4	0%	100%
4 and less than 5	40%	60%
5 and less than 6	45%	55%
6 and less than 7	50%	50%
7 and less than 8	60%	40%
8 and less than 9	70%	30%
9 and less than 10	80%	20%
10 and less than 11	90%	10%
11 or more	100%	0%

For any Plan Year during which the Plan is a Top-Heavy Plan (as defined in Article VIII), the Plan Administrator shall calculate a Participant's Vested Percentage of his Employer Contribution Amount in accordance with the following schedule:

Vesting Schedule		
Years of Service	**Vested Percentage**	**Forfeited Percentage**
Less than 2	0%	100%
2 and less than 3	20%	80%
3 and less than 4	40%	60%
4 and less than 5	60%	40%
5 and less than 6	80%	20%
6 or more	100%	0%

Total Plan Assets as of 10/31/00: $111,111.11

Plan Federal Tax Identification Numbers: Profit Sharing Plan: 111-11-1111

Plan Sponsor: XYZ Company, Inc.

Trustees

The persons ultimately responsible for making all decisions regarding the administration of XYZ Company, Inc., including the management of plan assets, and for carrying out this Investment Policy Statement on behalf of the plan as a "fiduciary," shall be the Trustees of the plan. The Trustees are:

President/Chief Financial Officer

Investment Management

The Trustees shall appoint investment managers to manage certain assets of the Plan. No more than 65% of the plan assets shall be under the management of any one Investment Manager. Each Investment Manager shall acknowledge by separate letter that they shall be a "fiduciary" as defined in Section 3(21)(A) of ERISA for that portion of the Plan's assets it is managing.

Investment Managers (including mutual funds and limited partnership sponsors) shall be chosen on the basis of their previous track record in the investment category for which they are being considered. Investment Managers and their track records shall be compared with appropriate broad market indices and with other comparable managers providing similar services and expertise. The Trustees shall consider only those money managers and mutual funds who can provide audited investment results over the most recent one, three, and five-year periods. Investment Managers with audited 10-year track records will be given preference where such experience is available and performance is at least comparable.

Investment Managers shall be registered with the U.S. Securities and Exchange Commission and shall provide an updated ADV Part II to the Trustees annually, no later than March of each year.

Fiduciary Bonding: LMN Company
($1,000,000.00 limit)

Overview Commentary

XYZ Company, Inc., is in the restaurant business doing business. The company has been in business since 1971. Management believes that sales, income, and the number of company employees will remain the same for the next five years. With that in mind, it is the intent of the Trustees that investments are selected for their long-term investment results and that minimal consideration is given to short-term volatilities.

Contributions to the plan are expected to exceed any required distributions in each of the next five years. Contributions have been made at the level of 6.2% eligible payroll and are expected to continue at that level, resulting in $50,000 being contributed to the plan for 2000. Contributions are expected to remain approximately the same each year thereafter.

Economic Outlook

It is the anticipation of XYZ Company, and its investment managers that the U.S. economy will generally grow at moderate levels throughout the next decade, with occasional downturns and subsequent rebounds. Foreign economies, on average, are expected to grow at somewhat faster rates.

Investment Objectives

The primary investment objective for plan assets is to seek growth with only a minimum concern for income, while at all times maintaining reasonable liquidity to fund any required distributions. The specific investment objective of the plan shall be to achieve an average annual rate of return equal to the Consumer Price Index plus 4.5% for the aggregate investments of the plan, evaluated over a period of five years.

It is anticipated that 95% of the time performance results for the plan assets shall range in any single year from –5.5% to 21.0%, with an estimated mean return of 9.5%. Under "worst case conditions," plan assets shall be designed to lose no more than 5.5% in any single year or the composite indices of the portfolio. The Trustees agree, understand, and accept that there can be deviations from this objective and will evaluate performance over a five-year period. For the purposes of planning, the time horizon for investments is to be considered longer than ten years.

The Trustees of the plan have identified the additional objective as follows:

1. Safety is a concern of high order. The Trustees shall seek to minimize the year-to-year volatility of investment results. At the same time, the Trustees also recognize that they must accept a certain amount of volatility (risk) in order to achieve their desired investment return. To achieve this combination of requirements (lower risk with attractive returns), the plan assets shall be invested in a well-diversified manner.

2. The Trustees expect that their return objectives shall afford the plan participants with improved purchasing power in the value of their assets. The identified rate-of-return objective has been selected with the consideration of improved purchasing power in mind.

3. The Trustees recognize that in a profit sharing plan the participants bear the ultimate risk for how well the plan investments perform. Therefore, the Trustees acknowledge their responsibility to participants to act with prudence and to attempt to achieve competitive returns while avoiding undue risk.

Asset Category	Current Allocation	Target Allocation
Stock, Bonds, & Cash Under Asset Management	90%	90-100%
Non-Liquid Investments	10%	0-10%

Asset Allocation Performance Monitoring

It is the determination of the Trustees that plan asset managers determine the percentage of assets in each asset category is the best approach to minimize volatility while increasing the opportunity for long-term growth of the profit sharing plan portfolio and purchasing power for the participants.

The Trustees shall review the results of all investments on a quarterly basis. In such a review, they shall consider the performance of each Asset Manager against comparable market indices. Where the performance of any particular Asset Manager is significantly less than anticipated (as compared to other asset managers with comparable objectives) and less than the comparable market indices for the risk taken, the Trustees shall request from that Asset Manager a written report as to why the poor results occurred and what their recommendation for action, if any, might be.

Frequency of Review

The Trustees recognize that all investments go through cycles and, therefore, there will be short periods in which the long-term investment objectives are not met. The Trustees therefore establish a goal of achieving the stated investment return objectives over any five-year period. Thus, any changes in assets and managers will not be made until said assets or managers have at least five years to prove their ability. However, if any manager resigns or significantly changes the management style previously held, a change should be considered.

In reviewing the performance of investments, calculations shall be done on a basis of net-asset value performance.

Liquidity

The policy of the XYZ Company, Inc., Profit-Sharing Plan is to make funds available to vested employees at the nearest entry date one year after termination of employment. At that time, any vested funds shall then be made available to the former employee. This one-year lapse in time affords the profit-sharing plan the luxury of being able to plan more than adequately for its liquidity needs. Therefore, it is the judgment of the Trustees that liquidity needs to provide payment of vested funds to former employees shall be minimal, except as specifically arises. In other words, monies shall be set aside as a reserve for payment to terminated vested employees only as required for known transactions.

To maintain the ability to deal with unplanned cash requirements that might arise, the Trustees hereby determine that a minimum of 1.0% of plan assets shall be maintained in cash or cash equivalents, including money market funds or short-term U.S. Treasury bills. In addition to this amount, any claims to be paid to terminated employees for vested requirement amounts shall be added to this 1.0% nine months after the termination of said employee. The Trustees anticipate that annual funding generated by the employer's contribution to the profit-sharing plan shall provide the cash required of this section.

Marketability of Assets

Due to the Trustees' long-term investment horizon and their ability to provide for vested benefits to terminated employees from the cash balances and annual contributions, the Trustees have determined that, as appropriate, up to 10% of plan assets can be invested in illiquid, long-term investments. Such investments may include limited partnerships, private-party loans (except as restricted by law), venture-capital opportunities, leases and mortgages.

Diversification

A. Permitted investment categories

Investment of the profit-sharing plan funds shall be limited to the following categories:

1. Cash and cash equivalents, including money market funds;

2. Bonds (corporate, U.S. Government, or foreign government);

3. Bank certificates of deposit;

4. Stocks (U.S. and foreign-based companies);

5. Mortgages (individual, direct, and pooled funds);

6. Real estate;

7. Natural resources;

8. Equipment and property leasing.

B. Minimum Number of Investment Categories

At all times there must be a minimum of three investment categories represented among the plan assets.

C. Concentration of Investment Categories

At no time shall any investment category as listed in A above, represent more than 60% of all assets in the profit-sharing plan except in the case where capital preservation is the short-term objective; then 100% cash and cash equivalents is premitted.

No specific asset (an individual stock, an individual mortgage, an individual bond, or individual investment of any other type) shall be permitted to represent more than 10% of the aggregate assets of the plan.

The Trustees agree, accept and understand that they are fiduciaries of XYZ Company, Inc., Profit-Sharing Plan.

Adopted by the below-signed fiduciaries of the XYZ Company, Inc., Profit-Sharing Plan at _____ this _____ day of _____ .

_____

President
XYZ Company, Inc.

_____

Chief Financial Officer
XYZ Company, Inc.

_____

Trustee

_____

Trustee

Chapter 9

INVESTMENT MANAGEMENT PROCEDURES

ERISA does not differentiate between large and small plans when mandating investment management procedures. (There is no industry standard for defining small and large plans.) Studies have found that more than 80 percent of the smaller pension plans are not in full compliance with the prudent procedures previously outlined.[14]

There is a wide disparity in the expertise of persons holding themselves out as counselors and the quality (and cost) of services they provide. One of the most important qualities an investment counselor must prove is independent advocacy for the interests of the plan.

If an investment counselor can represent only a small handful of money managers, it is difficult to believe that the counselor can reach an unbiased decision about which managers are the most appropriate for the plan. To ensure that the interests of the counselor and the plan remain aligned, the investment counselor should be compensated only by the plan, based on the services provided.

ERISA does not differentiate between those plans that can "afford" expertise and those that cannot. ERISA holds all plans to the same level of fiduciary responsibility.

Notes:

[14] "Changes are Needed in the ERISA Audit Process to Increase Protection for Employee Benefit Plan Participants," Department of Labor- Office of Inspector General (Nov. 1989)

Chapter 10

DIVERSIFICATION OF PLAN ASSETS

It is an investment axiom that diversification is the key to reaching long-term goals, yet this area is one often violated by pension plans. While ERISA does not specify recommended percentages among asset classes, diversification is the only prudent action a fiduciary can take to protect the long-term health of the plan.

Prudent Diversification Requirements:

> (...A fiduciary shall discharge his duties with respect to a plan solely in the interest of the participants and beneficiaries...):
>
> "(C) by diversifying the investments of the plan so as to minimize the risk of large losses, unless under the circumstances it is clearly prudent not to do so." (ERISA Sec. 404(a)(1)(C))

Lack of diversification has been an easy target for litigation since (1) it is easier to prove than specific imprudence,[15] and (2) once a plaintiff proves lack of diversification, the burden shifts to the fiduciary (defendant) to demonstrate that non-diversification was prudent under the circumstances.[16]

The DOL regulations define diversification as a mechanism for reducing the risk of large losses. No further definition is provided. Diversification is a separate and distinct legal obligation from prudence. In an action for plan losses based on an alleged breach of the diversification requirements, the burden of proof is on the claimant to demonstrate that there has been a failure to diversify.

Satisfaction of the diversification requirement is usually determined based on all the facts and circumstances. If diversification is found not to exist, then the burden of justifying failure to follow this general policy is on the fiduciary. Congressional intent behind the diversification requirement is to protect a plan from serious loss due to economic hardship or natural catastrophe (i.e., fire, storm, earthquake, etc.). Of course, failure to diversify (e.g., a large cash equivalent position) may be prudent in the face of a declining or unstable market.

Example:

> *GIW Industries* allowed plan participants to allocate their account between one of three investment options. One option, selected by most participants nearing retirement, invested 70 percent of assets in long-term government bonds. The court determined that this violated the diversification requirements of ERISA since investment losses were not recovered by the time participant withdrawals began to take place. In this case, the court scrutinized the fiduciary's failure to inves-

tigate the plan's disbursement history and future funding obligations and the risk/return characteristics of long-term bond securities, subjecting the plan to significant imprudent cash flow risks. Burton & Jacobsen, Inc.[17]

The following should be considered when evaluating diversification of the plan's portfolio:

1. The amount of plan assets;

2. Type of investments (stocks, bonds, real estate, etc.);

3. Projected portfolio returns versus funding objectives;

4. Volatility of investment returns;

5. Liquidity and future cash flows;

6. Maturity dates and retirees' pension distributions;

7. Economic conditions affecting the company and plan investments;

8. Company and industry conditions;

9. Geographic distribution of assets;

There is not a specific minimum nor maximum for each asset class. ERISA states that a fiduciary should not invest an unreasonably large part of the funding in any one investment type. Interestingly, ERISA explicitly states a plan invested solely in bank CD's meets the diversification requirements. However, court cases seem to refute ERISA on this point (Blankenship v. Boyle).

A corollary to this is whether the fiduciary has considered enough comparable investments to ensure that the best alternative was chosen for the plan. This may involve a formal search for a money manager or a schedule of bond maturities with various qualities that correspond to future benefit payments. The fiduciary should be confident that enough alternatives have been reviewed to make the most suitable choice for the plan given inflation, comparable yields, risk versus return, etc. Choosing a local money manager merely for convenience will not suffice. A broad menu of choices that fit the plan's goals should be reviewed and a rationale given for choosing (or not choosing) certain investments.

Significant diversification advantages can be achieved with a small number of well-selected securities, representing different industries and having other differences in their qualities. Broadened diversification may lead to additional transaction costs, at least initially, but the constraining effect of these costs can generally be dealt with quite effectively through pooled investing. Since optimal diversification may require participation in large portfolios, a professional trustee may be required to use pooled investments in certain circumstances.

Notes:

[15] Marshall v. Teamsters Local 282 Pension Trust Fund, 485 F.Supp 986 (E.D. NY 1978); Freund v. Marshall & Ilesly Bank, 485 F. Supp 629 (W.D. Wisc. 1979); Brock v. Berman, 673 F.Supp 634 (D.C. Mass 1987); Donavan v. Guaranty National Bank, 4 E.B.C.1686 (S.D. W. Va. 1983); and Brock v. Citizens Bank of Clovis, 841 F.2d 344 (10th Cir. 1988) but cf. Withers v. Teachers' Retirement System of the City of New York, 447 F.Supp 1248 (S.D. NY 1978); Sandoval v. Simmons, 622 F.Supp 1174 (D.C. Ill. 1985) and Davidson v. Cook, 567 F.Supp 225 (E.D. Va. 1983), aff'd mem., 734 F2d 10 (4th Cir. 1984).

[16] H.R. Rep. No. 1280, 93rd Cong., 2d Sess. 302 at 304 (1973).

[17] 10 E.B.C. 2290 (S.D. Ga. 1989) aff'd 895 F 2d 729 (11th Cir 1990).

Chapter 11

ASSET ALLOCATION

Diversification has evolved to include asset allocation. A number of studies have concluded that asset allocation decisions have the greatest impact on the overall long-term performance of a portfolio.

Asset allocation is not simply a pie chart illustrating, the categories of a portfolio. It should be a formal, ongoing recorded process based on the fiduciary's considered evaluation of each trust and the principles of modern portfolio theory. Intuition, unsupported conclusions and mere labels will not meet the standards of more recent standards of UPIA.

For any given expected rate of return, an optimal mix of asset classes could be determined that will yield the expected rate of return with the least amount of volatility or risk. Conversely, for any given level of assumed risk, a higher expected return may be obtained by mixing different asset classes than by investing in a single asset class.

Four variables enter into every asset allocation decision:

1. Time horizon of the portfolio;

2. Assumed risk tolerance or variability of returns;

3. Expected rate of return;

4. Selection of asset classes.

Once the four variables have been determined, computer-modeling tools (using simulated market conditions) can easily determine the portfolio's optimal mix. This optimal mix should then be incorporated in the plan's investment policy statement, consistent with the plan's investment goals and objectives.

The percentages can also be broken down to show how much money goes into each asset class. The concept known as Modern Portfolio Theory has helped in this process. Harry Markowitz won the Nobel Prize in Economics in 1990 for this contribution. He states that for every level of risk, there is some optimal combination of investments that will give you the highest rate of return. The range of portfolios exhibiting this optimal risk-reward trade-off form what we call "the efficient frontier", shown below. The efficient frontier is determined by calculating the expected rate of return and standard deviation for each asset class.

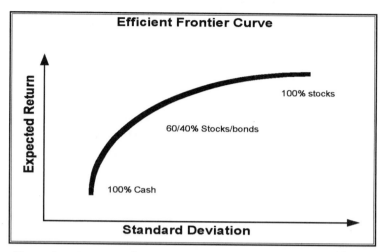

Efficient Frontier Curve

By plotting each percentage combination of the various asset classes, we are able to view the efficient frontier curve. In this example, we see that a portfolio of 60% stock and 40 % bonds gives us a higher expected return than cash, without the volatility of 100 % stocks.

The objective when combing asset classes is to select ones that exhibit low correlation to one another.

Portfolios That Have A Negative Co-Variance: The Two Portfolios Move Inversely

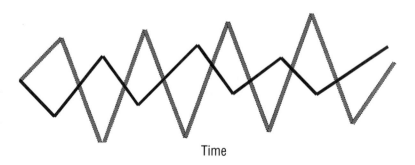

Time

The concept is to select asset classes that do not move lockstep with one another as the financial markets change. In statistical terminology, this implies a low *correlation coefficient*.

The purpose of asset allocation is to create an insulating effect around your entire portfolio so it doesn't move up or down quickly or harshly. This will give you a more consistent return over any long term period – a 5, 10, 15, or 20-year time frame. Asset allocation can level the effects of volatility on the value of your portfolio.

Chapter 12

RISK MANAGEMENT

All investments involve some risks. Therefore, the duty of a fiduciary does not call for the avoidance of risk, but rather for the prudent management of risk. This requires that careful attention be given to a particular trust's risk tolerance; that is, to its susceptibility to volatility.

The degree of risk permitted for a particular trust is ultimately a matter for interpretation and judgment. It is important that fiduciaries make a reasonable effort to understand the levels of risk and the types of investments suitable to the fund.

Assumed risk tolerance or variability of return.

For investment purposes, risk is defined as the probability or likelihood of not attaining one's investment objectives within a given time period. Equities have an historical compounded return of approximately 10 percent, but are considered "risky" because the return the investor may actually receive in any given year can vary significantly from this mean.

Expected rate of return.

Once each asset class is selected (stock, bond, etc.), the fiduciary is required to determine the expected rate of return of that market, given the appropriate levels of risk. In other words, the choice must be made in the context of overall risk, and the investment choice should represent the "fair" return, not necessarily the "highest."

The fiduciary should set a realistic expected return that, at the very least, will ensure growth of assets over inflation. A fiduciary faced with investments of equal risk should not choose the one with the lower returns, if a higher return is available.

A common mistake fiduciaries make is to assume that the best way to avoid risk is to seek the safety of cash and/or fixed income securities. Over extended periods of time (e.g., 10 years) inflation can deteriorate the real return of a fixed income portfolio.

Chapter 13

PROHIBITED INVESTMENT TRANSACTIONS

The fiduciary cannot derive a current benefit from the use or management of retirement plans' assets.

A fiduciary with respect to a plan shall not cause the plan to engage in a transaction, if he knows or should know that such transaction constitutes a direct or indirect:

(a)   *sale or exchange, or leasing, of any property between the plan and a party in interest;*

(b)   *lending money or other extension of credit between the plan and a party in interest;*

(c)   *furnishing goods, services, or facilities between the plan and a party in interest;*

(d)   *transfer to, or use by or for the benefit of, a party in interest;*

(e)   *cause a plan to acquire and to retain employer securities or employer real property in violation of Section 407(a)." (ERISA Sec. 406(a)(1)(A)-(E)).*

Chapter 14

MONITORING AND EVALUATION

The delegation of plan asset management provides two specific benefits to the plan and its fiduciaries. First, it fulfills the obligation for exercising prudence as defined within the Prudent Expert Rule. Second, the fiduciary is not liable as a co-fiduciary for any acts or omissions of the investment manager as *long as the fiduciary maintains adequate oversight of the manager.*

It is critical to bear in mind that the fiduciary's responsibilities are ongoing and liability exists even when professionals (e.g., money managers) are hired and subsequently breach their fiduciary duties or fail to meet plan goals. In other words, delegation alone will not protect a fiduciary; a system of delegation and oversight will. This oversight obligation consists of regular monitoring and evaluating, which are facilitated via a systematic reporting procedure. These systems must be in place if a fiduciary is to fulfill its responsibility.

The process of monitoring should mirror the plan's funding and investment objectives.[18] Being able to evaluate past performance, service and plan policies is as important as the ability to facilitate future changes.

The following minimum standards should be considered when designing a monitoring process:

1. Establish the benchmarks or indices against which the manager will be judged;

2. Determine the appropriate time frame and frequency of review;

3. Compare real versus nominal return;

4. Measure return benchmarks in relation to risk benchmarks. (What if the manager's returns are slightly subpar, but risk elements are superior?);

5. Analyze manager performance relative to peers;

6. Define the degree of personal attention desired.

Chapter 15

THE INVESTMENT PROFESSIONAL

It is obvious from the foregoing discussion that the typical fiduciary will have difficulty in meeting many of ERISA's requirements without professional assistance.

ERISA encourages fiduciaries to use financial professionals, investment consultants and money managers. A money manager who is registered with the SEC is a registered investment advisor. While the fiduciary has the exclusive authority to manage plan assets, that authority can be delegated to a professional if the plan so provides in writing. Moreover, only a named fiduciary can delegate responsibility for management of plan assets:

> *"if an investment manager or managers have been appointed... no trustee shall be liable for the acts or commissions of such investment manager or managers, or be under any obligation to invest or otherwise manage any asset of the plan which is subject to the management of each investment manager." (ERISA Sec. 405(d)(1))*

The fiduciary should be aware of the fact that suitable money managers:

1. Must be registered with the SEC under the Investment Advisor's Act of 1940 (unless exempt, as would be the case for most banks and insurance companies);

2. Must acknowledge their fiduciary status in writing. Any professional providing advice must do so pursuant to a written agreement;

3. Should demonstrate their understanding of the plan objectives by reviewing or drafting a written Investment Policy Statement.

Types of Investment or Financial Advisors

The selection of an investment or financial advisor is an exacting process since it affords many vital considerations. Exactly who manages money — and how do they do it?

Banks

Banks are still trying to get into to this business aggressively, but may lack the experience. These institutions are abundant in number, existing in virtually every community. Nearly half of all smaller pension plans are managed by bank trust departments, their sponsors having selected them because of their own past associations with the bank. Broadening the relationship to include money management services seems both a wise and expedient thing to do. There may, however, be some underlying disadvantages, one of which is that, historically speaking, banks have had a tendency to under-perform. Also, their investment choices are frequently impeded or delayed by the need for committee approval which may prevent timely action. The investor, looking in from the outside, may not be in a position to evaluate a bank's performance in the proper light.

Example:

While a bank may be able to come up with some really good performance numbers on their balanced account (perhaps through the conscientious efforts of a rising SuperStar on the equity side of the ledger), the portfolio may show an extremely poor fixed income side, where another segment of the group is listlessly plodding along. The investor, who is concentrating on the balanced account, will not be in a position to see that the fixed income numbers are actually being "propped up" by the equity numbers, which is an important thing to know and certainly justifies close monitoring of the portfolio's performance.

Bank trust departments traditionally operate under "trust rules" which are not necessarily compatible with the new ERISA rules so ultimate benefits may not be realized. This is a handicap of bank trust departments. It is also important to remember that the bank's trust department generates revenue based on the assets customers entrust to them and charges the customer a percentage fee for taking control of their money. They are, of course, obliged to provide you with something to do with your money, although they would just as soon provide the services connected with rolling it over in

CDs and then re-loan the money and make additional money on the spread. But, for people who are interested in participating in some growth, the banks will provide money management services, primarily in order to appear accommodating.

Even so, most banks are not in the money management business. Rather, they are in the business of borrowing money from you and lending it out to somebody else at a higher price. Realistically speaking, banks are re-marketers of money as opposed to money managers. And again, we must emphasize that a bank is charging you to manage the money they are using.

Finally, banks may not have the requisite experience of other financial investment advisors.

Insurance Companies

Insurance companies, like banks, are expanding into the money management business, but they also may be too conservative or lack the experience. Unlike banks, which guarantee a full return on your investment only on FDIC insured products, insurance companies will guarantee a certain rate of return. They may place the money in a large commercial building, or use it to purchase some long-term bonds. Whatever their choice, you do not get to participate in the actual investment. They are investing your money for themselves. An insurance company will gladly pay you eight percent so that they can receive twelve. This method of investment is popular during periods of economic instability, when investors are more interested in a "safe" return than a highly profitable one.

A limiting factor is that most insurance companies provide only "fixed" rates of return, which today may not be appropriate. Finally, the primary disadvantage to utilizing an insurance company for money management purposes is its lack of individual account management and flexibility.

Mutual Funds

Current studies indicate that mutual funds and brokerage firms manage the largest share of small pension monies. Mutual funds are preferable for accounts that can't meet the minimum requirements of independent Money Managers. They can also provide low cost management and possess some of the industry's best investment talent. Mutual funds are appropriate for smaller plans because they provide a large number of choices. They offer great flexibility of features and benefits; they are low cost, provide professionally managed, turnkey sponsor programs for retirement plans, and are highly regulated with public reporting of performance.

Mutual funds are probably the closest thing available to professional money management, although they have some of the same problems as banks.

As a potential investor, it is sometimes difficult to decide which fund to buy. If no investment objectives have been established, it will be very difficult indeed, since every mutual fund is listed by objective. Today, since there are many different objective categories to choose from, it becomes necessary for the investor to categorize himself.

An important distinction is whether or not you're working with a financial advisor. Those who purchase funds directly will have no one in the way of a salesman or consultant to rely upon, and so, will need to determine on their own whether or not a given fund meets their particular investment requirements. Working with a financial advisor, one can expect professional help and guidance in devloping a prudent portfolio of mutual funds.

In cases where an investor is dealing with one of the larger banks or insurance companies, he may find himself confined to a very limited number of funds and in many cases, may only be offered a fund that is managed by the bank's or insurance firm's parent company.

Research services are a valuable resource to financial intermediaries and can help in the selection process. While there are services that will rank mutual funds for you, it is important to understand that all they are doing is ranking performance. They will not supply a complete breakdown or synopsis of everything and everyone involved since that is not what they are in business to do. And again, unless the advisor has made a concerted effort to closely monitor the company, he will not be in a position to pass along this vital information.

Independent Investment Management Firms

These are fast becoming the largest groups to offer investment services. They provide the most flexible and complete array of personalized investment services for the intermediate-sized pension sponsor. Generally, they are owned by investment professionals who offer individual account management. Their highly competitive nature encourages them to strive for superior performance and, because these professionals are frequently well compensated, the firms experience little in the way of personnel turnover.

Chapter 16

INVESTMENT MANAGEMENT CONSULTANT

An investment management consultant's job is to match a pension plan with an outside investment manager. He/she does this by first establishing realistic, long-term investment objectives with the following considerations: the plan's return expectations; the amount of assets desired to have under management; risk tolerance; income/cash flow needs; appropriate asset allocation; and time horizons for the funds.

The consultant checks the professional backgrounds and past performance records of money managers in order to properly evaluate and categorize them. This helps in narrowing down the most favorable candidates whose individual style most effectively complements the investment objective of the plan. The consultant will help a plan sponsor complete a detailed questionnaire covering topics such as income needs, time horizon risk tolerances, economic situation, and financial goals.

The information obtained from the questionnaire will be used to write an investment policy statement based on the plan's return expectation and the amount of risk they are willing to accept. This policy statement also serves as a written job description for the investment advisor or money manager.

What is the difference between a money manager and an investment management consultant?

A money manager buys and sells securities on his client's behalf. Their investment decisions are based on the manager's experience, training, and proven investment strategies in accordance with clearly stated investment objectives.

Investment management consultants do not directly manage plan assets. Consultants analyze plan objectives, help formulate a written investment policy document, establish appropriate asset allocations, introduce the plan sponsors to suitable money managers, monitor the plan's account, and evaluate the managers on an on-going basis.

Can a plan sponsor find a money manager on his/her own?

They can. But, if done properly, it is very time consuming, cost prohibitive, and requires skilled experience. While there are many databases available to the investment community, finding a money manager is an art requiring more than simply looking at marketing brochures or the data published in financial magazines.

Many investment management consultants are members of professional associations that have standards or examinations. The Institute for Investment Management Consultants (the Institute), which is a national non-profit professional association for the consulting profession, provides training development and continuing education for its members. The Institute awards the following designations for achievements in the field of investment management consulting:

1. AIMC (Accredited Investment Management Consultant) – This designation is granted to Institute members in good standing who have completed a detailed course in the process of investment management consulting. Subjects covered include: The development of investment policies; money manager analyses; asset allocation; performance monitoring and evaluation; and understanding ERISA (Employment Retirement and Income Securities Act of 1974).

2. CIMC (Certified Investment Management Consultant) — This designation is awarded to those Institute members who are seasoned in the consulting process and who meet several criteria developed by the Institute's Committee on Certification and Ethics. To earn the CIMC, a consultant must have five or more years as a registered representative of the New York Stock Exchange, or seven years of investment experience with no less than 25 separate consulting accounts and $15 million under management.

Questions to ask a consulting firm under consideration:

1. How long has the firm been in the consulting business?
2. Number of professional consulting support staff and number of full-time analysts designated to

conduct on-site manager visitations, account audits and due diligence?

3. In the firm's consulting history, how many managers have they thoroughly evaluated by face-to-face interviews (versus questionnaire mailing)?

4. How many of the managers in the consulting firm's database are audited on the manager's premises annually?

5. Is the firm's database proprietary and self-developed or purchased from some other database? There is nothing inherently wrong with either database, although self-developed may imply that the consulting firm has taken more time and energy to evaluate money managers.

6. Does the firm have any affiliation to the money manager? Does the consulting firm provide and/or sell information to money managers? Do the managers in the database have to pay to be in the consulting firm's database or purchase data from the consulting firm? This will uncover potential and obvious conflicts of interest.

It is important that you know all of the financial industry activities or affiliations your investment management consultant's firm has. This will help you to determine whether your consultant may face any potential conflicts of interest and what his level of commitment is to the services you desire.

Typically, an investment management consultant will fall into one of the following four categories: (1) representing a consulting group or department affiliated with a money management firm, (2) representing an independent firm with a broker affiliate, (3) representing an insurance company subsidiary, (4) representing truly independent consulting firms such as Callon, Frank Russell or SEI, for example.

Questions to ask of an individual consultant you are considering:

1. What professional credentials or designations do they hold? Examples: CIMC, AIMC, CFA, CIMA

2. How long has the consultant been providing investment management consulting services?

3. What percentage of the consultant's business is dedicated to providing consulting services to clients?

4. What consulting services are provided? Examples: individually tailored investment policy statements; manager search and selection; objective performance monitoring and manager evaluation reports.

5. Consulting client experience (number of consulting relationships)? Ask for references.

6. What types of accounts are consulted? Examples: pension plans; public funds; foundations and endowments; eleemosynar; Taft-Hartley; high net worth individuals.

7. What size accounts does the consultant handle?

Some investment management consultants focus primarily on servicing large, institutional investors, such as pension funds, which have $50 million in assets or more. Others specialize in "high net worth" individuals, foundations/endowments, small/medium size pension plans ($100,000 to $50 million).

8. What references does the investment management consultant have? You should ask your investment management consultant for references from clients whose situations and objectives are similar to your own. Ask your consultant how long most of his clients have been with him. If at all possible, try to get references from clients who have worked with a consultant for at least three to five years. Your consultant should also be willing to furnish references from other professional organizations. One good source is the Institute For Investment Management Consultants.

9. What types of money managers does the consultant recommend? Rather than selecting an individual investment manager who favors the latest fad, or the best return in the last quarter, investment management consultants select the managers who use a discipline or style that is most suitable to meeting the objectives established in your investment policy statement.

10. What are the monitoring and review procedures used by consultants?

11. How is an investment management consultant compensated, and how do they set their fees? The fees charged by investment management consultants vary greatly. Many consultants charge different fees depending on the size of the portfolio, the investment instruments used, and other factors.

12. Custodian of the assets? Assets are not held by the registered investment manager (money manager). Your assets should be held in an insured custodial account at the brokerage firm where your consultant is affiliated or in an insurance custodial account offered by banks or trust companies. The insured bank custodian or trust accounts protect you from fraud, embezzlement, financial failure and such. Obviously, it does not insure against market value loss or guarantee returns. In most cases, money managers only have authority to make the buy/sell decisions in your portfolio operating under the guidelines of your investment policy statement.

There are three major ways in which an investment management consultant is compensated: fees, commissions, or a combination of fees and commissions.

a) Fee-only: investment management consultants set fees based on a percentage of the value of assets under management, or according to a set hourly rate or flat fixed fee, and receive no other compensation for their services. Those investment management consultants, who offer basic hourly rates, charge from $75 to $300 an hour. Some investment management consultants charge a fixed fee, also known as a flat fee for their services. Depending on the complexity of the plan and the services needed, fixed fees start at $500.00 and go up from there.

b) Commissions: investment management consultants who derive any part of their income from commissions receive part of the funds you invest in a particular product or security, regardless of the investment results. If the investment management consultant does not charge a fee, he is likely to be receiving commissions from transaction decisions made by the investment managers he recommends.

c) Combination: Some investment management consultants use an "offset" fee structure, also known as "soft dollars" where the fee charged is reduced by the amount of commission. Using a commission to offset a fee may be entirely appropriate, as long as the relationship between an advisory company and the investment management consultant is fully disclosed.

Chapter 17

404(C) PLAN

A pension plan may provide for individual accounts and permit a participant or beneficiary to exercise control over assets in his or her account. This type of plan is sometimes referred to as an "ERISA Sec. 404(c) plan."

Under a 404(c) plan the participant or beneficiary shall not be deemed to be a fiduciary by reason of his exercise of control, and no person who is otherwise a fiduciary shall be liable for any loss or by reason of any breach, which results from such exercise of control."[19]

The subject of only one major court review, the ERISA section 404(c) regulations are already being strained by new developments in the marketing of participant-directed 401(k) plans. Here is a look at some of the current issues under the regulations.

Background

ERISA section 404(c) provides, quite simply, that if a retirement plan with individual participant accounts allows a participant (or beneficiary) to exercise control over the investment of his or her account assets, and if he or she does so pursuant to Department of Labor ("DOL") regulations, then the participant will not be treated as an ERISA fiduciary with respect to his or her account, and a fiduciary who follows the participant's investment directions will be relieved of liability for any resulting losses.

Final regulations were adopted in 1992. They are not mandatory, nor do they set any "minimum" fiduciary standards for non 404(c) plans. Consequently, failing to follow the regulations does not result in any automatic fiduciary violation. Practically speaking, however, not following the regulations may be a perilous undertaking for an employer who permits participants to manage their own investment accounts because the employer theoretically remains responsible for monitoring each investment decision on an ongoing basis for prudence and diversification and for overriding participant choices that do not meet those standards.

Because the investment climate has been so favorable since 1992, there has not been much litigation clarifying the scope of the regulations. The recent Unisys case gave an expansive reading to the protections available to fiduciaries under section 404(c), but it's too early to tell whether other courts will follow the 3rd Circuit's reasoning.

Compliance Issues

The regulations are not a "safe harbor." In order to get the protection of section 404(c), a plan sponsor must follow all of the terms and conditions of the regulations, including a few that are more "form" than "substance."

One consequence of this "formalistic" application of the regulations is that many employers who think that they adopted 404(c) plans may risk losing the protections of section 404(c) for relatively minor violations. Some of these technical requirements repeatedly come to our attention:

Minor failure in communications: major impact

In our experience, one violation appears to stand out above all others: failing to tell participants that the plan is intended to be a section 404(c) plan. The regulations require that participants be told this explicitly, including the fact that plan fiduciaries may be relieved of losses which are the direct and necessary result of participant investment directions. Failure to comply with this requirement often occurs when an employer purchases a "bundled" or "wrap" 401(k) product from a vendor. Even if the vendor promises the program is section 404(c) compliant (and many do not), responsibility for employee communications frequently is left to the employer.

Prospectus delivery requirements

A plan offering mutual funds is required to provide a copy of the most recent prospectus immediately before or immediately after a participant's initial investment, and upon request. Because of cost considerations, many fund sponsors prefer to deliver a prospectus only to those participants who actually invest in a fund option. Moreover, participants do not always exercise their right to request a prospectus before delivery, thus calling into question whether they can make an informed investment decision. It is partly to address this concern that certain fund families now offer a "summary" prospectus.

The section 404(c) regulations do not require that a revised prospectus be delivered to each participant annually, so long as it is available on request (to the same extent it is available to the plan itself). However, many employers require fund sponsors automatically to do so in order to avoid subjective questions as to whether participants continue to make informed decisions.

Anticipating changes in investment options

Plan sponsors who provide a menu of investment options may elect to change them from time to time, by adding or subtracting individual funds, changing to a different vendor, or changing the form of an investment option (e.g., from a mutual fund to a bank collective fund). Such changes can be an administrative headache if participants are required to make new investment elections each time a change occurs. Although the regulations clearly require participants to make an affirmative initial election with respect to any investment option, a mere change in the form of an investment option may not require a new election if the initial disclosure materials and election forms can be structured to anticipate the subsequent change without being so broad as to fail to provide sufficient information for a participant to make an informed investment decision.

Employer securities require extra effort

Although a company stock fund cannot serve as a core investment option because it is not diversified, section 404(c) relief is available to such funds if they comply with some extra rules.

Those rules require (1) passing voting and tender rights through to participants, (2) keeping information about participant holdings and exercise of voting-type rights confidential, and (3) telling participants about the procedures and the fiduciary who is responsible for maintaining confidentiality. In the past, the extra burden of complying with these requirements often caused outside 401(k) administrators to decline to include employer securities within the scope of their services. However, a more competitive marketplace has increasingly brought employer stock funds into bundled services arrangements.

New array of investment options

In 1992, the regulations assumed a relatively simple model for section 404(c) relief. A plan would offer a specific "menu" of at least three investment fund options (usually mutual funds or bank collective funds) chosen by fiduciaries. Participants would choose among those options every quarter. This model seems very old-fashioned from the vantage point of 1998 when plans routinely provided daily valuations and investment "switching" with respect to a wide array of investment options. Increasingly, plans are moving away from the investment menu model to offer participants even greater investment control. These changes in the investment structure of section 404(c) plans will require the regulations to stretch in ways unanticipated in 1992. Among these alternative structures are:

"Open option" or "universal option" plans

A small percentage (but the number is growing rapidly) of plans now permit participants to choose their own investment options without restriction. Sometimes this arrangement is an add-on (i.e., a self-directed brokerage account "option" in addition to the regular menu of pre-selected funds). However, some plan sponsors have elected to forego altogether the fiduciary burden of selecting and monitoring investment options.

When offering a "brokerage option" involving a pre-selected provider (typically as part of a bundled product including custody, record-keeping and brokerage services) the plan sponsor generally will retain fiduciary liability with respect to the quality (i.e., cost and "best execution") of brokerage services being provided. A plan will most often make a single provider available to participants. One question often raised in the open option or directed brokerage context is whether the broker representing an individual participant becomes a fiduciary with respect to the plan or is otherwise covered under the penumbra of section 404(c) as an "agent" of the non-fiduciary participant. The answer appears to be that section 404(c) offers no special protection to the broker. Whether the broker is a fiduciary will be determined by whether the broker is providing investment advice and/or managing the assets of the participant's account, or merely carrying out the participant's instructions.

Manager options, including asset allocation

An alternative arrangement which is growing in popularity is for a plan to incorporate specific investment manager services into the investment structure of the plan. In such cases, there may be no separate "outside" investment fund into which plan assets are transferred. Rather, each manager simply takes responsibility with respect to a specified portion of the plan's assets, based on participant directions, and in turn directs the plan trustee as to the investment of those assets. Because they typically do not involve commingling the assets of multiple plans, these arrangements generally are cost-effective only for larger plans or for certain portions of a plan's assets.

Other arrangements may take the form of an "asset allocation" program and/or a "fund of funds," under which a participant may select the manager and/or a specified management or asset allocation "style," with the manager then taking fiduciary responsibility over the investment of the participant's assets among several "outside" investment funds. The structure of these programs, both in terms of the services provided and the fees charged, are still in flux because they can raise difficult fiduciary and prohibited transaction issues.

Broad range of investment alternatives

To provide a broad range of investment alternatives, a plan must offer participants the opportunity to exercise control over investments that materially affect the potential return on assets. In addition, it must also allow participants to choose from at least three investment alternatives, each of which is diversified and has materially different risk and return characteristics.

Participants must exercise "control"

A participant must exercise control over assets in the account. Restrictions on the movement of assets in a government investment contract fund, offered under a 401(k) plan, to other funds, relieved participants of control over their assets.

Charges for reasonable expenses

A plan may charge the account of a participant or a beneficiary for reasonable expenses incurred in carrying out investment instructions. However, the plan must inform participants and beneficiaries of the actual expenses associated with their individual accounts.

Cap on expenses charged to participants can avoid discrimination problems

Participant-directed account plans that offer participants a choice between a limited investment option and an unlimited investment option should consider placing a maximum cap on the expenses charged to participants who choose the unlimited investment option in order to avoid violating the nondiscrimination rules. The failure to cap the assessed charge could lead the IRS to treat the option as discriminatory because generally only participants with large account balances, who tend to be highly compensated employees, can afford to pay large charges.

Fiduciary may reject investment instructions

Fiduciaries are generally obligated to comply with the investment instructions of a participant or beneficiary. However, a fiduciary may refuse to implement investment instructions that would result in a prohibited transaction or generate income taxable to the plan. In addition, a human resources company that was hired by an employer to establish a 401(k) plan for unionized employees of a plant it had recently acquired, did not breach its fiduciary duty when it temporarily deposited funds from the 401(k) plan of the employees' former employer into money market accounts rather than invest them pursuant to the employee's instructions, where it did not have appropriate documentation to invest the funds individually and where the employees suffered no damages.

Restrictions on frequency of investment instructions

A plan may impose reasonable restrictions on the frequency with which participants may give investment instructions to the plan administrator. To be considered reasonable, the restrictions must offer participants the right to give investment instructions with appropriate frequency, considering the market volatility of the investment. For the three core investments, which are intended to constitute a broad range of investment alternatives, participants must be allowed to give investment instructions at least quarterly.

Opportunity to exercise control requires information

Participants will be considered as exercising control over their accounts only if they are provided with enough information about the plan and available investment alternatives to be able to make informed investment decisions. Items that must be provided to participants include:

1. An explanation that the plan is intended to comply with ERISA Sec. 404(c) and to generally relieve the fiduciary of liability for losses resulting from participants' investment directions;

2. A description of the investment alternatives, including a general description of the investment objectives and risk and return characteristics of each alternative;

3. Identification of any designated investment managers;

4. An explanation of the circumstances under which participants and beneficiaries may give investment instructions and of any limitations placed on those instructions set forth in the plan;

5. A description of any transaction fees or expenses which are charged to the participants' accounts;

6. The name, address, and phone number of the fiduciary who is responsible for providing certain documents upon request (see below) and a description of those documents;

7. In the case of plans that offer an investment alternative designed to permit a participant or beneficiary to acquire or sell any employer security, a description of the procedures relating to the confidentiality of information regarding the purchase, holding, and sale of the securities and to the exercise of voting rights; and the name, address and phone number of the fiduciary responsible for monitoring compliance with the procedures;

8. A copy of the most recent prospectus provided immediately prior to or immediately following a participant's initial investment in a mutual fund or security in which he or she has no assets invested; and

6. Subsequent to an investment, any materials provided to the plan relating to the exercise of voting, tender or similar rights (which are incidental to the ownership interests held in the account) to the extent that the rights are passed through to the participant, and a description of or reference to plan provisions describing those rights.

An employer should consider conducting a series of meetings to help ensure that ERISA Sec. 404(c) participants are adequately informed of investment options.

Additionally, certain information must be provided on request to participants, including a description of the annual operating expenses, of investment alternatives, copies of any prospectuses, financial statements and reports, and a list of assets comprising the portfolio of an investment alternative.

A fiduciary may be relieved of liability for investments in qualified employer securities if, among other things, procedures are established to ensure the confidentiality of participant investment information and a plan fiduciary is designated to review and monitor compliance with the procedures.

Election effective until affirmatively revoked

As long as transfer opportunities are made available to participants and beneficiaries in accordance with the regulations, an investment election remains in effect until it is affirmatively revoked by the participant or beneficiary. However, the investment instructions of a missing participant need not be followed if doing so would be imprudent (see below).

Investments in collectibles

Note that amounts invested in collectibles under a self-directed account in a qualified plan or under an IRA are treated as distributions for income tax purposes. Collectibles include antiques, art, rugs, metals, gems, stamps, coins, and alcoholic beverages. However, an exception applies to certain coins acquired by IRAs.

SIMPLE plans relieve employer of fiduciary liability

An employer maintaining a SIMPLE plan, or other plan fiduciary is relieved of fiduciary liability from actions taken by participants or beneficiaries who exercise control over assets in the SIMPLE account. A participant or beneficiary will be treated as exercising control over account assets once the account has been established for one year, or, if earlier, once an affirmative election regarding the initial investment of contributions is made, or a rollover contribution (including a trustee-to-trustee transfer) to another SIMPLE account or IRA is executed.

The Conference Committee Report to P.L. 104-188 notes that, once a participant or beneficiary is treated as exercising control over the SIMPLE account, the relief from fiduciary liability covers the period before the individual was deemed to exercise control.

Fees are not prohibited

Employers maintaining a SIMPLE plan are not specifically prohibited by the enacting legislation from assessing a fee with respect to a participant's initial decision regarding the investment of contributions. Nor are employers prohibited from imposing a reasonable fee based on the rate of return realized by assets in the SIMPLE account.

Corrective payments may cover certain investment losses

Amounts contributed to a qualified plan in excess of the applicable limits under Code Sec. 404 and 415 subject the plan to disqualification and the employer to penalty tax. However, corrective payments made by an employer to participants in a participant-directed retirement plan to compensate them for losses incurred following an investment in derivatives and to resolve potential resultant claims for breach of fiduciary duty, did not constitute contributions. Accordingly, the corrective payments would not subject the employer to the excise tax on nondeductible contributions and would not cause the plan's disqualification. The employer could not deduct the contributions, but the participants would not be currently taxed on the payments.

Insufficient information may trigger fiduciary liability

Generally, a plan trustee breaches its fiduciary obligation to a participant in a participant-directed plan only if the participant is denied control over his or her account. The failure of plan trustees to provide participants with adequate investment information would effectively deny the participants control over their accounts.

The information provided to participants may not be too general, but must be sufficient for the average participant to understand and assess all of the available investment alternatives. The fact that participants are presented with a wide variety of investment options does not guarantee that they possess control over account assets sufficient to shield the employer from fiduciary liability. Accordingly, in a case arising before the effective date of governing ERISA Reg. §2550.404(c), an employer could not avoid liability for losses sustained by participants investing in guaranteed investment contracts offered by a company that subsequently became insolvent, without proving that it provided information to the participants regarding their rights under ERISA, the consequences of exercising control over their accounts, the fiduciary obligations imposed on the employer, the financial condition and performance of investments, and developments materially affecting the financial status of the investments.

Participant-directed account plans that offer limited partnerships as an investment choice may encounter difficulty in providing participants with sufficient information to satisfy the requirements of ERISA Sec. 404(c)(2). There is not a ready source of information about limited partnerships comparable to the quarterly reports and prospectuses that are available to investors in mutual funds.

Investment education and fiduciary liability

Participants and beneficiaries in a 404(c) plan must have access to sufficient information to enable them to make informed investment decisions. ERISA Sec. 404(c) does not require a plan sponsor to provide investment advice or educational information, materials, or programs to participants in order to preserve its exemption from fiduciary liability.

If adequate investment education is provided, the potential for fiduciary liability should, as a practical matter, be limited. Further, if the ERISA § 404(c) rules are satisfied, 401(k) sponsors should have a defense to employee claims – so long as the investment options are properly selected and monitored.

Notes:

[19] Investment Company Institute "Investment Advisers Guide" which was most recently updated in September 1999.

Chapter 18

401(K) PLANS

When the era of employees working at the same company for 40 years ended and people started to change jobs more often, defined contribution plans, such as the 401(k), gained popularity as more appropriate retirement vehicles.

The 401(k) plan would allow individuals to place pre-tax contributions into special investment accounts not tied to an employer, and the money would grow tax-deferred until withdrawn during retirement. Employers could also contribute to the employee's account, which was a great way for them to offer an additional benefit while drastically reducing both the cost and liability associated with traditional pension plans.

Every new corporation started a 401(k) because there was no liability. Plus, they didn't have to worry about calculating retirement benefits. The new rule under the 401(k) was, "Whatever you have, you have." This forced the investment decision-making process onto the individual—an admirable idea, but it resulted in uninformed people making investment decisions that could have a profound impact on their financial futures.

These newly empowered employees, like the first wave of pension plan administrators, put all their money into fixed-income investments because they were thought to be safe. In the early days of 401(k) plans, 80 percent of employee contributions were invested in money market funds and bond funds.

That started to change when mutual funds launched intense advertising campaigns aimed at the 401(k) market. Suddenly, retirement plans were offering eight percent loaded funds to investors, a strategy that was easy for plan sponsors because the mutual fund was the easiest way to handle all the record-keeping responsibilities.

Next, Fidelity Investments started selling to the 401(k) markets and was able to eliminate sales loads. Educational campaigns were started to get people to invest in equity funds, which made more money. And then the greatest bull market in history began, and investors came to the conclusion that mutual fund returns would keep going up, up, and up.

These plans are basically qualified profit-sharing plans with additional features that make them more attractive in light of recent tax reform changes. The features give plan sponsors greater flexibility in making contributions, may allow participants greater involvement with investment decisions, and, may allow participants to make additional contributions of their own. However, the fiduciary should be aware of caveats.

Since a 401(k) plan is a form of profit-sharing plan, the fiduciary has complete discretion over the contributions made to the plan each year. Often contributions are linked to a formula based on the profits of the firm. Allocations to participants are required to be a uniform percentage of compensation in order to avoid discrimination favoring highly compensated participants.

The 401(k) may also be used with other qualified plans, subject to overlapping participant deductible amounts and annual contribution limits. This feature is attractive to plan sponsors that have fully funded defined benefit plans and/or desire a qualified plan that would involve greater employee participation.

The 401(k) may, at the discretion of plan sponsors, allow participants to choose the investment objectives (asset allocation mix) for their account. This is a popular option for plan sponsors because of the perception that the sponsor's fiduciary liability for making imprudent investment decisions would be reduced.

The fiduciary, however, should not be lulled into neglecting the other prudent procedures outline in this handbook. Money managers must still be prudently selected, supervised and monitored. The fiduciary is still responsible to ensure that each and every participant makes a prudent investment decision based on the participant's time horizon, risk tolerance, and return expectations.

Chapter 19

SUMMARY

ERISA (Employee Retirement Income Security Act of 1974) hasn't changed a lot since 1974, although there have been some exemptive orders (class exemptions) and court cases that clarified the Act.

The protection of employee benefit plan participants under ERISA is forthright, but the Department of Labor has realized that rules without compliance are meaningless. Increasing surveillance and audits of small and medium-sized plans are inevitable. It has been estimated that approximately eighty percent of small plans (those with assets under $3 million) are currently in violation of ERISA regulations. The role of the plan sponsor will intensify in the near future and an extensive understanding of ERISA is going to be key to long-term success in this area.

We do not hold ourselves out to be specialists in pension legislation, nor are we attempting to offer any legal advice. We do advise employers to deal with their retirement plan consultants, attorneys, or CPAs if they have specific questions regarding their retirement funds.

Financial advisors and intermediaries would be well served to follow the guidelines in this book and reduce the number of plans that are in non-compliance. This is a good business practice, an opportunity for the financial intermediaries to "add value," and a good public

Chapter 20

APPENDIX A — SUPPLEMENT TO A MANAGEMENT AGREEMENT

service to protect members of the public.

This Supplement applies only to Clients for which XYZ Co. has been appointed as an investment manager of any portion of the assets of a plan and related trust governed by the Employee Retirement Income Security Act of 1974 ("ERISA"), (collectively, the "Plan") by the Trustees of the Plan (the "Trustees").

The term "Client" in this Supplement shall include the Trustees. If the "named fiduciary" (as defined in ERISA) of the Plan, who is authorized to appoint a Money Manager as investment manager, is defined by a term other than "Trustees," then all references to "Trustee" and "Client" herein shall include such fiduciary. In the event of any inconsistency or conflict between this Supplement and any other terms or provisions of the Agreement, then this Supplement shall control.

1. The Client and/or their Investment Professional are responsible for notifying Money Manager that the Client is subject to ERISA.

2. The Client hereby represents to have full power, authority and capacity to execute the Money Manager Investment Management Agreement (the "Agreement"). If the Agreement is entered into by a Trustee or other fiduciary, including, but not limited to, someone meeting the definition of "fiduciary" under ERISA or an employee benefit plan subject to ERISA, such Trustee or other fiduciary represents and warrants that the Client's participation in XYZ Co's program is permitted by the relevant governing instrument of such plan, and that the Client is duly authorized to enter into this Agreement. The Client agrees to furnish such documents to the Money Manager as required under ERISA or as the Money Manager reasonably requests. The Client further agrees to advise the Money Manager of any event or circumstance which might affect this authority or the validity of this Agreement. The Client additionally represents and warrants that (i) its governing instrument provides that an "investment manager" as defined in Section 3(38) of ERISA may be appointed and (ii) the person executing and delivering this Agreement on behalf of the Client is a "named fiduciary", as defined under ERISA, who has the power under the Plan to appoint an investment manager.

3. The Money Manager further acknowledges that, in regard to those clients for which it serves as an "investment manager," it shall be a "fiduciary", as defined in Section 3(21)(A) of ERISA, for that

portion of the Plan's assets it is managing.

4. The Client agrees to obtain and maintain, for the period of this Agreement, the bond required for fiduciaries by Section 412 under ERISA and to include the Money Manager among those covered by such bond.

5. The Client has read, fully understands and agrees to be bound by the terms and conditions of the Agreement currently in effect, and as may be amended from time to time.

6. The Trustees acknowledge that they are responsible for the diversification of the Plan's investments and the Money Manager does not have any such responsibility.

Risk Disclosure Statement

XYZ Co. provides investment services to meet varying investment needs and risk tolerance. Clients should carefully consider whether such an investment is suitable in light of their financial condition. Prior to authorizing the Money Manager to invest for their account, the Client should carefully review the selected investment services. Should their objectives change, Clients should reevaluate their participation in these investment services and notify the Money Manager in writing of any change.

Any investment program entails the risk of loss. While we make every effort to keep these losses small, there have been numerous loss periods in the past and there will be others in the future. It must be stressed that investment returns, particularly over shorter time horizons, are highly dependent on trends in the various investment markets. XYZ's investment management services are suitable only as long-term investments, and should not be viewed as short-term trading vehicles.

If the Client is subject to ERISA, the Client hereby agrees to be bound by the terms of the 'ERISA Supplement to the Agreement.'

_____   _____

Client Signature   Date

GLOSSARY OF INVESTMENT TERMINOLOGY

The *Association for Investment Management Research (AIMR) Performance Presentation Standards (AIMR-PPS)* are recognized as the leading industry standards for ethical presentation of investment performance results. Their list of investment terms have also become the industry standard, and uniform use of these terms is the accepted norm. The AIMR-PPS standards promote fair representation and full disclosure in every firm's presentation of its performance results to clients and prospective clients. The Standards and standard terms were designed to ensure uniformity in performance reporting so that results are directly comparable among investment managers and forms. Below is a list of terms that pertain to ERISA, based on the AIMR standards.

Active Management: A portfolio strategy that endeavors to provide additional returns by continually repositioning portfolios to take advantage of the most favorable opportunities.

Analysis: Process of evaluating individual financial instruments (often stock) to determine whether they are an appropriate purchase.

Analysts: Those in the business of recommending and studying securities.

Annual Interest Income: The annual dollar income for a bond or savings account is calculated by multiplying the bond's coupon rate by its face value.

Asset allocation: The decision as to how a customer should be invested among major asset classes in order to increase expected risk-adjusted return. Asset allocation may be two-way (stocks and bonds), three-way (stocks, bonds and cash), or many-way (i.e., value mutual funds, growth mutual funds, small mutual funds, cash, foreign mutual funds, foreign bonds, real estate, and venture capital).

Asset-backed Security: A public or private security issued to finance a portfolio of receivables independent of the financial status of the originator or issuer.

Asset-class: Assets composed of financial instruments with similar characteristics.

Asset-Class Investing: The disciplined purchase of groups of securities with similar risk/reward profiles. This strategy is based on valid academic research and its results are predictable rather than random.

Asset Mix: Investable asset classes within a portfolio.

Balanced Index: A market index that serves as a basis of comparison for balanced portfolios. The balanced index used in the Monitor is comprised of a 60 percent weighting of the S&P 500 Index and a 40 percent weighting of the SLH Government/Corporate Bond Index. The balanced index relates unmanaged market returns to a balanced portfolio more precisely than either a stock or a bond index would alone.

Basis Point: One basis point is 1/100th of a percentage point, or 0.01 percent. Basis points are often used to express changes or differences in yields, returns, or interest rates. Thus, if a portfolio has a total return of 10 percent versus 7 percent for the S&P 500, the portfolio is said to have outperformed the S&P 500 by 300 basis points.

Benchmark: A standard by which investment performance or trading execution can be judged. The most widely used performance benchmark is the total return of the S&P 500.

Beta: Beta is the linear relationship between the return on the security and the return on the market. By definition, the market usually measured by the S&P500 Index, has beta of 1.00 Any stock or portfolio with a higher beta is generally more volatile than the market, while any with a lower beta is generally less volatile than the market.

Bottom-Up Analysis: An approach to valuing securities that first involves analyzing companies, then the industry, and finally, the economy.

Cap: Small Cap, Large Cap: The stock market worth of an individual equity. Large-cap stocks can be found on the New York Stock Exchange. Small cap stocks are often listed on the NASDAQ.

Correlation: A statistical measure of the degree to which the movement of two variables is related.

Certified Financial Planner (CFP): Federally-registered trademarks, the CFP and Certified Financial Planner designations are used by individuals who have met, and continue to meet, the education, examination, experience, and ethical requirements established by the Certified Financial Planner Board of Standards for the practice of financial planning.

Chartered Financial Analyst (CFA): A designation awarded by the Association for Investment Management and Research (AIMR) to experienced financial analysts who pass examinations in economics, financial accounting, portfolio management, security analysis, and standards of conduct. Many investment managers have this designation.

Certified Investment Management Consultant (CIMC): A designation awarded by the Institute of Investment Management Consultants (IIMC) to experienced consultants who have met the stringent criteria and pass NASD-administered examinations on pertinent topics including Principles of Portfolio Management, The Consulting Relationship, Ethics, Asset Allocation, Investment Policies, and Performance Monitoring. CIMC's specialize in working with high-net worth individuals, qualified plans, business owners, and institutions.

Convertible Bond: A bond that may, at the holder's option, be exchanged for common stock. Convertible bonds offer the downside floor price of a "straight" bond while potentially allowing the holder to share in price appreciation of the underlying common stock. This conversion feature makes it possible for the bondholder to convert the bond to shares of the issuer's common stock.

Core Investment Strategy: A core investment strategy is one that forms the foundation of an investors portfolio – one that is generally conservative in nature and has as one of its primary focuses the generation of above market returns with below market risk.

Current Yield: The annual interest on a bond divided by the market price. The current yield is different from the yield to maturity in that it uses the actual income rate as opposed to the coupon rate.

Deviation: Movement of instrument or asset class away from expected direction. In investment terminology, most often associated with asset-class analysis.

Dissimilar Price Movement: The process whereby different asset classes and markets move in different directions.

Direct Brokerage: Circumstances in which a board of trustees or other fiduciary requests that the investment manager direct trades to a particular broker so that the commissions generated can be used for specific services or resources.

Disbursement: Any net decrease in the level of funding for a portfolio, asset class, or security.

Dividend Yield: The current annualized dividend paid on a share of common stock, expressed as a percentage of the stock's current market price.

Dow Jones Industrial Average (DJIA): A price-weighted average of 30 leading blue-chip industrial stocks, calculated by adding the prices of the 30 stocks and adjusting by a divisor, which reflects any stock dividends or splits. The Dow Jones Industrial Average is the most widely quoted index of the stock market, but it is not widely used as a benchmark for evaluating performance. The S&P 500 Index, which is more representative of the market, is the benchmark most widely used by performance measurement services.

Due Diligence: Process of checking and verifying information. Ensuring that sufficient analysis has been conducted before making or recommending an investment or investment advisor to a client.

Duration: A measure of the average maturity of the stream of interest payment of a bond. Duration is always shorter than maturity, except for zero coupon bonds.

Efficiency: The process of generating maximum reward from funds invested across a spectrum of asset classes.

Efficient Frontier: The point where the maximum amount of risk an investor is willing to tolerate intersects with the maximum amount of reward that can potentially be generated.

Efficient Market: A theory that claims a security's market price equals its true investment value at all times, since all information is fully and immediately reflected in the market price.

Efficient Portfolio: A portfolio that offers maximum expected return for a given level of risk or minimum risk for a given level of expected return.

Equal Weighted: In a portfolio setting, this is a composite of a manager's return for accounts managed that gives equal consideration to each portfolio's return without regard to size of the portfolio.

Employment Retirement Income Security Act (ERISA): A 1974 law governing the operation of most private pension and benefit plans. The law eased pension eligibility rules, set up the Pension Benefit Guaranty Corporation, and established guidelines for the management of pension funds.

Emerging Growth: This implies new companies that may be relatively small in size with the potential to grow much larger.

Expected Return: Calculated as the weighted average of its possible returns, where the weights are the corresponding probability for each return.

Fiduciary: Indicates the relationship of trust and confidence where one person (the fiduciary) holds or controls property for the benefit of another person.

Foundations and Endowments: Charitable institutions, many with substantial pools of assets, founded with the express intention to fund worthwhile programs and research.

High Yield: A fixed income investment strategy where the objective is to obtain high current income by investing in lower rated, higher default-risk, fixed-income securities. As a result, security selection focuses on credit risk analysis.

Income Return: A measure of the gain or loss of a security or portfolio due only to income earned and the change in income accrued.

Index: A statistical composite that measures changes in the economy or financial markets. Stock market indices are unmanaged and reflect the value of different segments of the U.S. stock market. Well-known U.S. indices include the Dow, and the S&P 500.

Index Fund: A passively managed investment in a diversified portfolio of financial assets designed to mimic the performance of a specific market index.

Institutional Investor: Pension funds, foundations, endowments, investment companies, bank trust departments, life insurance companies, all of whom oversee large portfolios of securities.

Intrinsic Value: The underlying value of a stock, as determined through fundamental analysis.

Investment Policy Statement (IPS): A written document describing financial goals, how capital will be invested, the target date for the accomplishment of the goals, and the amount of tolerable risk. It should include: (1) assessing where your plan is now, (2) detailing where you want it to go, and (3) developing a strategy to get there.

Investor Discomfort: Realization that risk is not appropriate and reward is not predictable in a given portfolio.

Investment Philosophy: Strategy justifying short or long-term buying and selling of securities.

Investment Wisdom: Process of understanding valid academic research concerning asset allocation.

Liquidity: In general, liquidity refers to the ease by which a financial asset can be converted into cash. Liquidity is often more narrowly defined as the ability to sell an asset quickly without having to make a substantial price concession.

Load: The percentage commission or sales charge on mutual funds, insurance policies, etc.

Lump Sum Distribution: Single payment to a beneficiary covering the entire amount of an agreement. Participants in Individual Retirement Accounts, pension plans, profit sharing, and executive stock option plans generally can opt for a lump sum distribution when they become eligible if the taxes are not too burdensome.

Management Fee: Charge against investor assets for managing the portfolio of an open- or closed-end mutual fund as well as for such services as shareholder relations or administration. The fee, as disclosed in the prospectus, is a fixed percentage of the fund's asset value, typically 1 percent or less per year.

Market Return: The rate of return of the benchmark used for the attribution comparison for the time period analyzed. Typically, the S&P 500 Index is used as the benchmark.

Market Timing: This is defined as the attempt to base investment decisions on the expected direction of the market. If stocks are expected to decline, the timer may elect to hold a portion of the portfolio in cash equivalents or bonds. Timers may base their decisions on fundamentals (e.g., selling stocks when the market's price/book ratio reaches a certain level), on technical considerations (such as declining momentum or excessive investor optimism), or a combination of both.

Modern Portfolio Theory (MPT): An investment decision approach that permits an investor to classify, estimate and control both the kind and amount of expected risk and return. Essential to portfolio development when using MPT are the quantification of the relationship between risk and return and the assumption that investors must be compensated for assuming risk. This portfolio approach shifts emphasis from analyzing the characteristics of individual investments to determining the statistical relationship among the individual securities that comprise the overall portfolio.

Money Markets: Financial markets in which financial assets with a maturity of less than one year are traded. Money market funds also refer to open-end mutual funds that invest in low-risk, highly liquid, short-term financial instruments and whose net asset value is kept stable at $1 per share. The average portfolio maturity is 30 to 60 days.

Mutual Fund: Professionally managed Investment Company made up of co-mingled funds from multiple investors used to create a diversified portfolio of securities.

Mutual Fund Expenses: Internal charges that may be incurred by the investor in both load and no-load funds in addition to any sales fees.

National Association of Securities Dealers, Inc. (NASD): The principal association of over-the-counter (OTC) brokers and dealers that establishes legal and ethical standards of conduct for its members. NASD was established in 1939 to regulate the OTC market in much the same manner as organized exchanges monitor actions of their members.

Net Asset Value (NAV): This is defined as the market value of each share of a mutual fund. This figure is derived by taking a fund's total assets (securities, cash and receivables) deducting liabilities and then dividing that total by the number of shares outstanding.

Nominal Return: This is the actual current dollar growth in an asset's value over a given period. See also total return and real return.

No-Load: A mutual fund with no sales commission charge.

Optimization: A process whereby a portfolio, invested using valid academic theory in various asset classes, is analyzed to insure that risk/reward parameters have not drifted from stated goals.

Passive Management: For a given asset class, the process of buying a diversified portfolio that mimics the overall performance of the asset class.

Performance Attribution: The process of evaluating the factors that contribute to the total rate of return of a portfolio. Performance attribution is most commonly used in the monitoring of common stock portfolio performance, where breakdowns of sector performance are readily available for comparison.

Plan Sponsor: Parent organization of a benefit plan, such as an employer or nonprofit entity.

Portfolio Turnover: Removing funds from one financial instrument to place in another. This process can be costly.

Price/Earnings Ratio (P/E): This may be defined as the current price dividend by reported earnings per share of stock for the latest 12-month period. For example, a stock with earnings per share during the trailing year of $5 and currently selling at $50 per share has a price/earnings ratio of 10.

Price-to-Book Ratio: A measure of value for a company that is equal to the market value of all the shares of common stock divided by the book value of the company. The book value is the sum of capital surplus, common stock, and retained earnings.

Prudent Investor Rule: Officially named the "Uniform Prudent Investment Act," this standard of prudence was drafted by the National Conference of Commissioners on Uniform State Laws (1994) and has been legislated in a majority of states. Rooted in modern portfolio practices, the Prudent Investor rule emphasizes that an investment portfolio should be examined in its "totality" and that the results of a single investment can only be meaningfully evaluated against this macro framework. This Rule is similar to the Employee Retirement Income and Security Act (ERISA) legislated by Congress in 1974 to safeguard qualified retirement plans.

Quartile: A ranking of comparative portfolio performance. The top 25 percent of mutual fund managers are in the 1st Quartile, those ranking from the 26 percent to 50 percent are in the 2nd Quartile, from 51 percent to 75 percent in the 3rd and the lowest 25 percent in the 4th Quartile.

Qualified Plan: Tax-deferred plan set up by an employer for employees under 1954 IRS rules. Such plans usually provide for employer contributions that are paid out at retirement or on termination of employment. The employees pay taxes only when they draw the money. When employers and employees make payments to such plans, they receive certain deductions and other tax benefits.

Real Estate Investment Trust (REIT): An investment fund whose objective is to hold real estate-related assets, either through mortgages, construction and development loans, or equity interests.

Relative Return: The return of a stock or a mutual fund portfolio compared with some index, usually the S&P 500. For example, in 1989, American Brands had a total return of 12.2 percent in absolute terms. In isolation, that sounds good. After all, the historical annualized return on common stocks has been 10.3 percent. But because the S&P 500 had a return of 31.7 percent in 1989, American Brands underperformed the index in relative terms by 19.5 percentage points. Thus, its relative return was -19.5 percentage points.

Rebalancing: A process whereby funds are shifted within asset classes and between asset classes to insure the maintenance of the efficient frontier. See optimization.

Real Return: This is the inflation-adjusted return on an asset. Inflation–adjusted returns are calculated by subtracting the rate of inflation from an asset's apparent, or nominal, return. For example, if common stocks earn a total return of 10.3 percent over a period of time, but inflation during that period is 3.1 percent, the real return is the difference: 7.2 percent.

Risk: Risk is nothing more than the uncertainty of future rates of return, which includes the possibility of loss. This variability or uncertainty causes "rational" investors to expect higher returns on investments where the actual timing or amount of payoffs is not guaranteed. A mutual fund portfolio has two types of risk. The first, called market risk captures the amount of portfolio variability caused by events that have an impact on the market as a whole. The second is business risk, which are fundamental company risks.

Risk Tolerance: Investors' innate ability to deal with the potential of losing money without abandoning investment process.

Risk-adjusted Return: The return on an asset or portfolio modified to explicitly account for the risk of the asset or portfolio.

Russell 2000 Index: An index of stocks composed of the 2000 smallest stocks in the Russell 3000 Index. (The Russell 3000 Index consists of the 3000 largest U.S. securities as determined by total market capitalization.) The largest company in the index has an approximate market capitalization of $745 million.

Securities and Exchange Commission (SEC): The keystone regulator body engaged in the regulation of securities markets. It governs exchanges, over-the-counter markets, broker-dealers, the conduct of secondary markets, extension of credit in securities transactions, the conduct of corporate insiders, and principally the prohibition of fraud and manipulation in securities transactions. The Securities and Exchange Commission has the power to interpret, supervise, and enforce the securities laws of the United States.

Securities Investor Protection Corporation (SIPC): This is a government-sponsored organization created in 1970 to insure investor accounts at brokerage firms in the event of the brokerage firm's insolvency and liquidation. The maximum insurance of $500,000, including a maximum of $100,000 in cash assets per account, covers customer losses due to brokerage house insolvency, not customer losses caused by security price fluctuations. SIPC coverage is conceptually similar to Federal Deposit Insurance Corporation coverage of customer accounts at commercial banks.

S&P 500 Index: An index of stocks composed of the 500 largest companies in the U.S. The index is market weighted, which means the larger the company, the larger the weight in the index. The index is widely used as a stock benchmark for account performance measurement. This index includes 400 industrial stocks, 20 transportation stocks, 40 financial stocks, and 40 public utilities. Performance is measured on a capitalization-weighted basis. The index is maintained by Standard & Poor's Corporation, a subsidiary of McGraw-Hill Inc.

S&P Common Stock Rankings:

The S&P rankings measure historical growth and stability of earnings and dividends. The system includes the following rankings:

A+, A, and A-	Above average
B+	Average
B, B- and C	Below average
NR	Insufficient historical data or not amenable to the ranking process.

As a matter of policy, S&P does not rank the stocks of foreign companies, investment Companies, and certain finance-oriented companies.

Standard deviation: Volatility can be statistically measured using standard deviation. Standard deviation describes how far from the mean historic performance has been, either higher or lower. Mean is simply the middle point between the two historic extremes of the performance of the investment you are examining. The standard deviation measurement helps explain what the distribution of returns likely will be. The greater the range of returns, the greater the risk. Generally, the current price of a security reflects the expected total return of its investment and its perceived risk. The lower the risk, the lower the expected return.

Strategic Asset Allocation: Rebalancing back to the normal mix at specified time intervals, or when established tolerance levels are violated.

Style: The description of the type of approach and strategy utilized by an investment manager to manage funds. (See Chapter Six for investment styles.)

Tactical Allocation: Investment strategy allocating assets according to investor expectations of directions of regional markets and asset classes. Certain indicators make adjustments in the proportions of the portfolio invested in three asset classes: stocks, bonds and cash.

Technical Analysis: Any investment approach that judges the attractiveness of particular stocks, or the market as a whole, based on market data, such as price patterns, volume, momentum, or investor sentiment, as opposed to fundamental financial data, such as earnings dividends.

Top-Down Analysis: Securities analysis that forecasts

broad macro-economic trends, then assesses the impact on industries, and finally, on individual companies.

Third Restatement: Legislation based on the "Third Restatement of Trusts" adopted by the American Law Institute that suggests individual investment decisions should be made in the context of the total portfolio. Fiduciaries are required to properly diversify assets so as to minimize the potential for large declines in the value of the total portfolio. (See Prudent Investor Rule.)

Time Weighted Rate of Return: The rate at which a dollar invested at the beginning of a period would grow if no additional capital were invested and no cash withdrawals were made. It provides an indication of value added by the investment manager, and allows comparisons to the performance of other investment managers and market indexes.

Total Return: A standard measure of performance or return including both capital appreciation (or depreciation) and dividends or other income received. For example, Stock A is priced at $60 at the start of a year and pays an annual dividend of $4. If the stock moves up to $70 in price, the appreciation component is 16.7 percent, the yield component is 6.7 percent, and the total return is 23.4 percent. That oversimplification does not take into account any earnings on the reinvested dividends.

Transaction Costs: Another term for execution costs. Total transaction costs (or the cost of buying and selling stocks) have three components: (1) the actual dollars paid to the manager in commissions, (2) the market impact—i.e., the impact a manager's trade has on the market price for the stock (this varies with the size of the trade and the skill of the trader), and (3) the opportunity cost of the return (positive or negative) given up by not executing the trade instantaneously.

Turnover: Turnover is the volume or percentage of buying or selling activity within a mutual fund portfolio relative to the mutual fund portfolio's size.

Underperform: Securities or markets that do not meet expectations.

Value stocks: Stocks with high book to market valuations—i.e., companies doing poorly in the market that may have the potential to do better.

Value Added: These are returns over and above those of the stock market.

Volatility: The extent to which market values and investment returns are uncertain or fluctuate. Another word for risk, volatility is gauged using such measures as beta, mean absolute deviation and standard deviation.

Yield (current yield): For stocks, yield is the percentage return paid in dividends on a common or preferred stock, calculated by dividing the indicated annual dividend by the market price of the stock. For example, if a stock sells for $40 and pays a dividend of $2 per share, it has a yield of 5 percent (i.e., $2 divided by $40).

For bonds, the coupon rate of interest divided by the market price is called current yield. For example, a bond selling for $1,000 with a 10 percent coupon offers a 10 percent current yield. If the same bond were selling for $500, it would offer a 20 percent yield to an investor who bought it for $500. (As a bond's price falls, its yield rises, and vice versa.)

Yield to maturity: The discount rate that equates the present value of the bond's cash flows (semi-annual coupon payments of the redemption value) with the market price. The yield to maturity will actually be earned if (1) the investor holds the bond to maturity and (2) the investor is able to reinvest all coupon payments at a rate equal to the yield to maturity. When a bond is selling at par, the yield to maturity and the coupon rate are equal.

Yield curve: A chart or graph showing the price of securities (usually fixed income) through time. A flat or inverted yield curve of fixed income instruments is thought by many to be an indicator of recession. This is because those who borrow at the far end of the curve usually pay more for their money than those who borrow for only a little while. When the yield curve is flat or inverted this means there is little demand for long-term money and this can be interpreted as a signal that there is little demand in the economy for the products that long-term borrowing would generate.

401(k) section of the Internal Revenue Code: In its most simple terms, a 401(k) plan is a before tax employee saving plan.

BIBLIOGRAPHY

Invest According to ERISA: John R. Lohr, Isle Press, West Chester, PA, 1987.

"Assessing Risk Tolerance Levels: A Prerequisite to Personalizing and Managing Portfolios," Financial Analysts Journal, Jan.-Feb. 1989, pgs. 14-16.

Federal Supplement, Department of Labor vs. Miller Druck Company, Inc. Employee Stock Ownership Plan, United States District Court, S.D. New York, March 7, 1988.

Fiduciary Responsibilities Under ERISA, Kirk F. Maldonado, Stradling, Yocca, Carlson & Rauth, Newport Beach, CA, Fall 1986.

"How to Select a Consultant for Your Fund," Financial Analysts Journal, Jan.-Feb. 1989, pgs. 4-7.

Investment Advisors Act of 1940, U.S. Securities and Exchange Commission, Division of Investment Management, Washington, D.C.

Service Providers as Fiduciaries Under ERISA, Jonathan S. Kitchen, Baker & McKenzie, San Francisco, June 1989.

Using ERISA to Develop New Business; John R. Lohr, Isle Press, West Chester, PA, 1987.

"Columns," Reed Smith Shaw & McClay, Virginia, Aug. 2000

Procedural Prudence for Fiduciaries, 1997, by Donald B. Trone and William R. Allbright and The Management of Investment Decisions, Irwin Professional Publishing, 1995, by Donald B. Trone, William R. Allbright and Philip R. Taylor.

This book, along with other books, are available at discounts that make it realistic to provide them as gifts to your customers, clients, and staff. For more information on these long lasting, cost effective premiums, please call John Boyer at 800-424-4550 or email him at john@traderslibrary.com.

ABOUT THE AUTHOR

Ken Ziesenheim is currently Managing Director of Thornburg Investment Management, the manager and advisor for Thornburg Mutual Funds and serves as President of Thornburg Securities Corporation, the distributor of Thornburg Funds.

Prior to joining Thornburg in 1995, Ken was Senior Vice President of Mutual Fund Marketing at Raymond James &Associates.

Ken holds a degree in Business Administration from Stetson University, a Juris Doctor from Baylor University, and a Master of Law in Taxation from the University of Denver. In addition, he is a Certified Financial Planner and a Certified Mutual Fund Specialist.